A TOURIST GUIDE TO
CIVIL WAR
Washington D. C.

Thomas Power Lowry M.D.

HISTORY BOOKS BY THE AUTHOR

Idle Winter Press
Portland, Oregon
http://IdleWinter.com

This edition published 2017
Printed in the United States of America
The text of this book is in Alegreya

ISBN-13: 978-1945687037 (Idle Winter Press)
ISBN-10: 1945687037

A TOURIST GUIDE TO
CIVIL WAR
Washington, DC

Thomas Power Lowry, MD

Idle Winter Press
Portland, Oregon

CONTENTS

ACKNOWLEDGEMENTS

The legendary Michael P. Musick introduced me to the records of the provost marshal. Beverly A. Lowry created the court-martial database which can find obscure subjects in milliseconds. Vital help in census records related to prostitution came from an esteemed colleague who has drawn a veil of modesty over his professional identity.

Special thanks to those foresighted individuals who preserved our nation's records, and a final salute to all those men and women 150 years ago, whose bones are now dust, but whose lives live on in paper, pen, and ink.

INTRODUCTION

It is a timeless story. Unattached young men, loose in a new city. Not just this century, or last century, but as far back as we can imagine.

"Hi, centurion; new to Damascus?" "Hello, esteemed Crusader, salaam; first time in Alexandretta? Food? Wine? A girl?" Or in any millennium: "Hi, there soldier boy. Lookin' for a good time?" And later they even sang of their novel experiences: "How're you going to keep 'em down on the farm, after they've seen Paree?"

The maritime equivalents are legend. "New in town, sailor?" The men who staggered back onto their ship, penniless, after "spending money like a drunken sailor," were often, in their own words, "stewed, screwed, and tattooed." A classical sea chantey asks the question, "What shall we do with the drunken sailor, early in the morning?" (The answer, of course, is "Put him in the scuppers with the hosepipe on him.")

Then there are the melancholy chords of loneliness and longing, the pangs of separation, expressed so poignantly in:

> Under 'neath the lamppost, by the barracks gate,
> Standing all alone, you will see her wait.
> Lili Marlene. Lili Marlene.

No eye remains dry, whether those words are brought to us by pathos of Edith Piaf or the sultry phrasing of Marlene Dietrich. On the other side of the world, Rudyard Kipling's "Mandalay" tells of yet another lonely man and his distant love.

> By the old Moulmein Pagoda, lookin' lazy at the
>   sea,
> There's a Burma girl a-settin', and I know she
>   thinks of me;
> For the wind is in the palm-trees, and the
>   temple-bells they say;
> Come you back, you British Soldier; come you
>   back to Mandalay!

In a more modern era, we see the traditional greeting of legendary "Tex" Guinan—"Hello, suckers!" While her notorious 300 Club in New York's prohibition years catered to Vanderbilts and Whitneys, with drop-ins such as Mae West, "Tex" embodied the spirit of giving the customer what he wants, and taking his money.

However, our focus in this work is not the European wars, or the reaches of empire, or the conflicts of antiquity, but our own orgy of self-destruction, the American Civil War, and the city of Washington, DC, as experienced by the tens of thousands of young soldiers who passed through its streets and alleys in the years 1861-1865.

Washington DC is a strange town. It is both a capital of international importance and a hotbed of small, quarreling neighborhoods. It is clearly not Yankee, yet not part of the Magnolia dream of the Deep South. It has been described, with wry humor, as "A city of Northern charm and Southern efficiency," by both Senator Warren Magnuson and John F. Kennedy. In 1860 Washington DC had unpaved streets (a few cobblestones on Pennsylvania Avenue), with clouds of dust in the summer and deep mud in winter, and a population of 75,000. In 1870 Washington DC had unpaved streets, with clouds of dust in the summer and deep mud in the winter, and a population of 131,700. While it still lacked the amenities of London or Paris, DC had nearly doubled in population. The 1870 figure was five years after the troops had marched home; at the height of the war an unknown number swelled the city.

Wartime Washington DC has been written about before. Margaret Leech's *Reveille in Washington* won the Pulitzer Prize in 1942. In 419 pages of text and sixty pages of bibliography and index, she told a wonderful story of the doings in the years 1861-1865. Her book is still the perfect introduction to that wartime city. Two *caveats*: individual tales are not footnoted, therefore Leech's book is of little use to historians, and, secondarily, she was married to Ralph Pulitzer.

The author has added to the stories of Washington DC in his *The Stories the Soldiers Wouldn't Tell* (1994) and *Primrose Path* (2011), originally published as *Capital Courtesans.*

This present work brings to light the original records of the provost marshal of Washington DC. The city had a municipal police department which was to protect the civilian population. The provost marshal was to regulate the behavior of soldiers and their officers. The provost sent out teams of inspectors and enforcers, whose duties were to keep tabs on the city's numerous saloons, restaurants, hotels, bordellos, and gambling establishments. To aid them in their work the provost created a hand-written database of all these places, with addresses, proprietors, and quality rating. It's important to note that when the provost guard visited saloons and houses of prostitution, they arrested only men who were there without passes or who had turned violent. Just being drunk and/or in a whorehouse was not an offense in itself. In addition, the provost called upon all the saloon owners to sign a pledge that they would not serve alcohol to soldiers. (It was all right to serve the officers.)

One final thought before looking at the old records. By 1863 the glamor and glory of war was but a distant memory. The reality was loneliness, wounds, disease, and death. The order of the day was Eat, Drink, and make Merry, for Tomorrow We Die, the same admonition voiced by Ecclesiastes (8:15) 2,300 years ago.

The *corpus* of this book is transcripts of the hand-written original records. They provide a unique picture of what the visiting soldier (or tourist) would find in our nation's capital during the Civil War.

CHAPTER 1
HOTELS AND RESTAURANTS

———————————

The first document in the provost marshal's file of social activity in the capital is a listing of hotels and restaurants. It appears to be in no particular order, either by type of establishment or by location, except that all are on Pennsylvania Avenue, always shortened to "Pa. Ave." The numeration (one through sixty) is exactly as in the original. The usual sequence in each entry is: name of establishment; street address; name of proprietor; and character of the establishment. "Char." appears as an abbreviation for "character." A few entries have a note such as "3rd class." The full range of classes is discussed in detail in the chapter "Patterns."

Some of the distinctions are hard to clarify at this distance in time. What is the difference between a "drinking house" and a "drinking saloon?"

A few terms have changed and evolved over the 150 years, most notably the meaning of "saloon." In most American minds it evokes the saloon in a Western cowboy movie: the double swinging doors, the character actor behind the bar making pithy comments, and men in big hats playing poker. The 1856 Webster's Unabridged Dictionary has this to say: "**Saloon.** In architecture a spacious and elegant apartment for the reception of company or for works of art. It is often vaulted at the top and frequently comprehends two stories, with two ranges of windows. It is a state room much used in palaces for receptions of ambassadors and other visitors. The term is also applied to a large room on a steam boat." Although written only five years before the Civil War, it does not sound much like the saloons encountered by the young soldiers of the war.

The 2016 *Oxford English Dictionary* tells us an updated version. "A public room or building used for a specified purpose. Examples might be billiard saloons or beauty saloons. In North America it is used in an historical or humorous context as a place where alcoholic drinks may be bought or sold." (One senses the British looking down their noses at the uncouth Yankees.)

The term "grocery" also merits attention. The 1856 Webster's defines "grocery' as the items sold by a grocer, "a trader who deals in tea, sugar, spices, coffee, liquor, fruits, etc." In our reading of thousands of Civil War courts-martial we saw the term usually used to designate a place where bottled whiskey was sold. In a final culinary note, several establishments mention oysters and/or lager beer. Today, due to disastrous overfishing and polluted water, non-poisonous oysters are a luxury for the rich. In 1863, the vast oyster beds of the Chesapeake Bay made these delightful mollusks the food of the poor. As for lager beer, it is produced by methods perfected in the Late Middle Ages by German-speaking brewers, fermented and matured in the chill of caves and ice houses. Today, cold brewing is the dominant method of production. Now to the provost marshal's list.

1. Eagle Restaurant. 171 Pa. Ave. H.C. Wistorf, Prop. Char. Good.
2. Jas. McGranns Restaurant. 179 Pa. Ave. between 17th and 18th Streets. Char. Good.
3. St. Nicholas Hotel. Pa. Ave. Corner F Street. John McEntosh, Prop. Char. Good.

4. J. D. Hammack's Restaurant. Nos. 200 & 202 Pa. Ave. Char. Good.

5. Markhams Restaurant & Hotel. 212 Pa. Ave. Markham & Henderson, Props. Char. Good.

6. Willards Hotel. Corner 14th St. and Pa. Ave. Chadwick. Char. Good.

7. Gautier Restaurant. 252 Pa. Ave. Eating & Drinking Saloon. G. Gautier, Prop. Char. Good.

8. Kirkwood House. Corner 12th & Pa. Ave, J.H. & H. M. Kirkwood. Char. Good.

9. Metropolitan Hotel. Pa. Ave, between 6th & 7th Streets. A. R. Potts. Char. Good.

10. Dulants Eating & Drinking Saloon. Corner Pa. Ave. & 6th. T.M. Dulant & Bro. Char. Good.

11. National Hotel. Pa. Ave. between 4th & 6th Streets. F. Tenney & Co. Char. Good.

12. C. Tovinelli Eating & Drinking Saloon. 428 Pa. Ave. Char. Good.

13. Pullmans Hotel. Pa. Ave. between 3rd & 4 ½ Streets. W. Pullman [Rullman?]. Char. Good.

14. United States Hotel. Pa. Ave. between 3rd and 4 ½ Streets. N.H. Beam & Co. Char. Good.

15. Columbia Hotel. 484 Pa. Ave. George A. Springman. Char. Good "as far as known."

16. Washington House. Pa. Ave. & 3rd St. Mrs. A.F. Beveridge. Char. Good.

17. St. Charles Hotel. Corner Pa. Ave. & 3rd St. Seth Lamb. Char. Good.

18. St. Charles Restaurant. Corner Pa. & 3rd St. Eating and Drinking Saloon. T. Craigin. Char. Good.

19. Columbia Restaurant. 512 Pa. Ave. Eating and Drinking Saloon. Jos. Platz. Char. Good.

20. P. Heddesheimer Lager Beer Restaurant. 516 Pa. Ave. Char. Apparently good.

21. Chas. Heisler. Drinking and Eating Saloon. 532 Pa. Ave. Char. Apparently good.

22. McManns Eating and Drinking Saloon. 536 Pa. Ave. A Resort for Soldiers.

23. Capitol House. 546 Pa. Ave. Eating & Drinking Saloon. E. Suisson [?] & A. Zona. Char. Good as far as known.

24. Steels Restaurant. Drinking & Oyster Saloon. [no address recorded] James Steel. Char. Good as far as known.

25. E. Lagore. Eating & Drinking Saloon. 570 Pa. Ave. Corner 17th [?] St. Char. good as far as known.

26. New York Lager Beer Saloon. 534 Pa. Ave. Francis Englis. Char. orderly as far as known.

27. Union Refectory. S West corner Pa. Ave. & 3rd St. Eating & Drinking Saloon. Chas. Meidis. Char. Good as far as known.

28. F. Ochland Lager Beer Saloon. 449 Pa. Ave. Char. Apparently Good.

29. Chas. Nichols. Restaurant. 403 Pa. Ave. Char. Apparently Good.

30. Clinton Hotel. 429 Pa. Ave. Drinking Saloon. W. Hackery. Char. Apparently Good.

31. Geo. McHees Eating Saloon. 415 Pa. Ave. Char. Good as far as known.

32. Arlington House. Corner Pa. Ave. & 4 ½ St. J. H. Moore. Char. Good as far as known.

33. [?] McCafferey. Steamed Oyster Saloon. 397 Pa. Ave. Char. Good as far as known.

34. Monitor Hotel. 391 Pa. Ave. Chas. Ruebles. Char. Good as far as known.

35. Murrays Hotel. 367 Pa. Ave. B. Murray. Char. Good as far as known.

36. Clarendon Hotel. Corner Pa. Ave, & 6th Street. T. Norris. Char. Good as far as known.

37. Central Hotel. Corner Pa. Ave. & 6th Street. H.D. Gelston. Char. Good as far as known.

38. Mrs. Warner Eating & Drinking Saloon. 355 Pa. Ave. Char. not known.

39. A. Mut. Confectionary & Eating Saloon. 374 Pa. Ave. Char. not known.

40. Delevan House. 317 Pa. Ave. Mrs. Bates. Char. not known.

41. Academy of Music. Concert & Drinking Saloon. 289 Pa. Ave. Rosenthal & Broncis. Char. Good as far as known.

42. Simpson House. Corner 10th & Pa. Ave. Mrs. Simpson. Char. Good as far as known.

43. Ice Cream & Drinking Saloon. 279 Pa. Ave. Thos. Potentinis. Char. Good.

44. J. Russell Dining Saloon. 277 Pa. Ave. Char. Good as far as known.

45. Franklin Hotel. 253 Pa. Ave. C. Fenickman. Char. Good as far as known.

46. M. Haymann. Eating & Drinking Saloon. 247 Pa. Ave. Char. Good.

47. The Relic. 239 Pa. Ave. A. Hancock. Char. Good.

48. Trescott House. 236 Pa. Ave. Barons & Hersche. Char. Good.

49. Browns Restaurant. Corner Pa. Ave. & 13th Street. J. Brown. Char. Noisy.

50. Farmings & Wens Saloon. Corner Pa. Ave. & 14th St. Char. Good as far as known.

51. Gillens Retreat. 225 Pa. Ave. John Gillen. Char. not known.

52. 1st Ward Steamed Oyster Saloon. 162 Pa. Ave. A. Woodley. Char. Good.

53. C. F. Sauers Restaurant & Drinking Saloon. 129 Pa. Ave. Char. Good.

54. Robt. Miller Grocery & Liquor Store. Corner Pa. Ave. & 1st Street. (East Capitol) Char. Low.

55. Fred Meyer. 75 Pa. Ave. Drinking House. 3rd Class. Char. Good as far as known.

56. Pennsylvania Hotel. 57 Pa. Ave. M.M. Wheelock. 3rd Class. Char. Good.

57. Andrew Lowry Restaurant (under Pa. Hotel). 4th class. Char. Good as far as known.

58. Isaac Perrman [Rerrman?] Circle House. 13th & Pa. Ave. 3rd class. Char. Good as far as known.

59. Bowman Rottely [?] Restaurant. 136 Pa. Ave. & 2nd [?] Street. 4th class. Char. Unknown.

60. Mrs. Hopkins Eating & Drinking Saloon. Corner Pa. Ave. & 6th Street. Char. Good.

CHAPTER 2
SOME GEOGRAPHY

The previous pages focused on Pennsylvania Avenue but there was much more to the District of Columbia: streets, alleys, and other avenues. The plan of the city was Enlightenment Rational, a neat north-south, east-west grid, with a few huge diagonal avenues, the 1792 product of the genius mind of Pierre L'Enfant. He was trained in classic art and architecture in Paris, served under Washington as a brevet major of engineers, and had a highly successful architectural practice in New York City.

L'Enfant chose as his central reference point Capitol Hill. He then set up four quadrants: northwest, southwest, northeast, and southeast. Then, as now, the northwest quadrant became the dominant section, politically and economically. The east-west streets were given letters, A Street, nearly non-existent, occupied a tiny area southeast of Capitol Hill. B Street, now Constitution Avenue, ran along the north bank of Tiber Creek, a body of water meriting special attention. After its banks were walled, it became Tiber Canal. Water runs downhill, and by 1860, every form of vile effluvia had been thrown into or washed into its fetid waters. When it was filled in and paved over, it was still the geographic low point and a great flood around 2005 filled the lower rooms of the National Archives.

Moving north, C street and D Street nearly disappeared in the massive redevelopment that became Federal Triangle, the area bounded by Pennsylvania Ave NW, Constitution Avenue NW, and 15th Street NW, but during the Civil War C and D streets had dozens of hotels, restaurants, and saloons. The provost marshal's records tell us of establishments from A Street all the way north to T Street.

The north-south streets were numbered, not lettered. Those in the northwest quadrant began with 1st Street at the foot of Capitol Hill and today extend west all the way to 45th Street.

Then there were the alleys. Within the blocks created by the numbered and lettered streets, there were narrow passages, largely occupied by African-American families, both as housing and as an extensive economy of small businesses. In the years from 1850 up until the First World War, the alleys contained an ever-evolving society with its own rules, benevolent societies, music, and jobs. Largely overlooked, indeed invisible in the usual histories, they seem to have been successful adaptations to a hard world, rather than passive and pitied ghettoes.

THE ISLAND

Many businesses are described as located on "The Island." A look at a section of the 1792 Thakara & Vallance map (next page) shows the Tiber Canal running along the northern edge of The Mall, then turning southeast at the base of Capitol Hill, to debouche into the Anacostia River. All the land south of the canal was referred to as The Island. It harbored a criminal element. The police went there only in pairs or small groups. Today the streets in that area usually carry a suffix of SW (southwest) but in the Civil War era the quadrant designators were rarely used.

Probably for the task of organized patrols of the military police, the provost marshal's office created a roster of the establishments on the lettered streets. Their number and diversity are remarkable. They certainly show that the visiting soldier or tourist would lack nothing in choices.

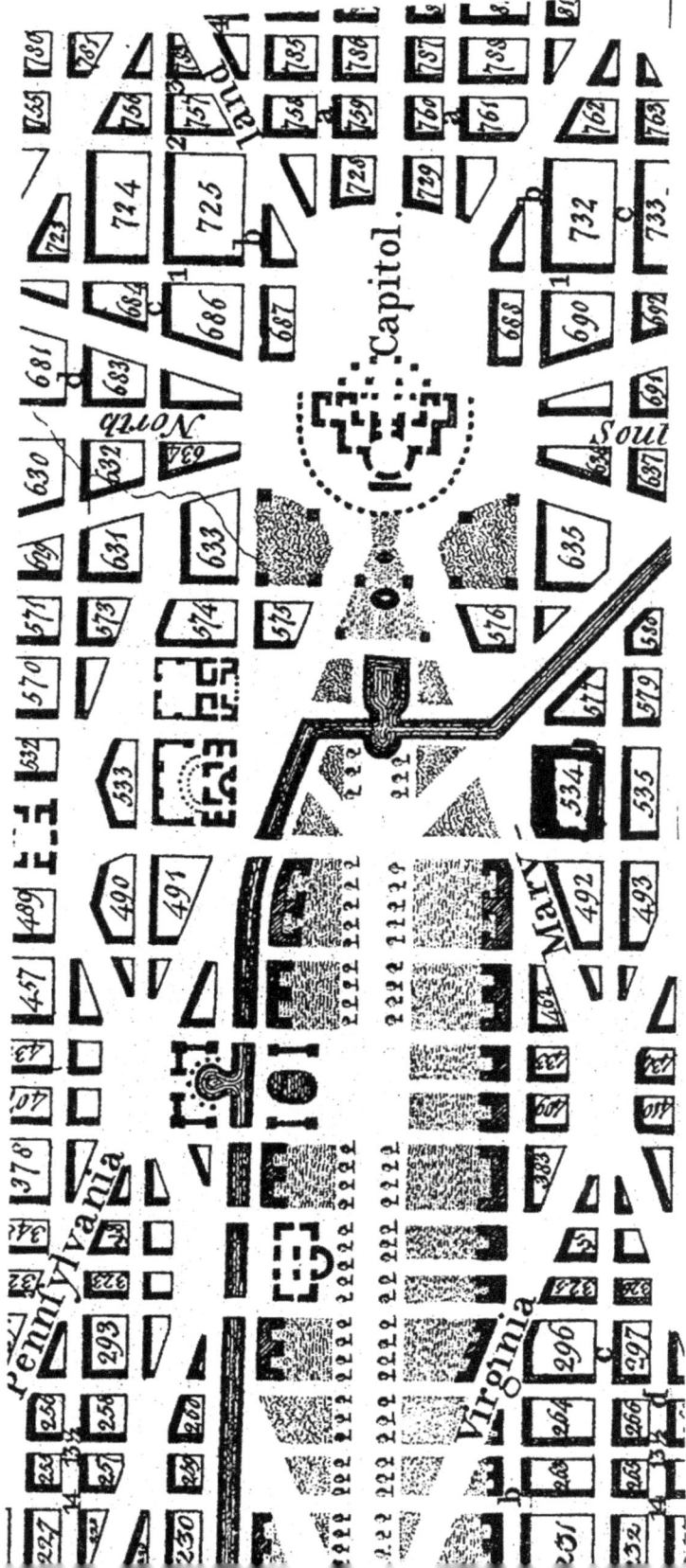

Capitol.

North

Sout

Pennsylvania

Virginia

Mar

730 731 732 733 734 735 736 737 738 8.

755 756 757 758 759 760 761 762 763

724 725 728 729 732 733

723 684 686 687 688 690 692

681 683 685 689 691

630 632 634 636 637

569 631 633 635

571 573 574 575 576 580

570 577 579

532 533 534 535

489 490 491 492 493

457 40

43 40

378 383

346 81

32 328 82

293 296 297

258 256 200 264 266 32

233 251 260 263

227 230 251 232

CHAPTER 3
COMMERCE ON LETTERED STREETS

These are arranged as follows: the name of the proprietor (last name first), the name of the establishment, the address, and any remarks. Many of the entries are in difficult hand-writing; transcription is as accurate as possible.

A STREET

- Hazel, John. White House. 5 South A St. 4th class.
- Whitney, Mrs. G.H. Restaurant. Corner of A St. and N.Y. Ave. South. 2nd class.

B STREET

- Sullivan, Patrick. Drinking saloon (low). Corner B & 1st Sts.
- Frere, James, Restaurant (Middleton). Corner B & 9th Sts.
- Warren, Mrs. Sophia. (low) 207 B St. near 6th.
- Juvenall, Jacob. Lager Beer & Liquor Saloon. Corner B & 6th Sts. 4th class.
- Haltzman, J. Restaurant. Island. Corner B & 6th Sts. 4th class.
- Marceron, M. Restaurant (South) Corner B & N.J. Ave. 4th class.
- Smith, F. National House. 337 B St. & E. Capitol. 3rd class.
- Moelich, F. Green Tree House. B St. between 2nd & 3rd St. 3rd class.
- McGrann, J. Grocery & Liquor. 287 B St. 3rd class.

C STREET

- Luts Saloon. Corner C & 6th Sts.
- Dugan, Felix. 292 C St. between 3rd & 4th Sts. Low class.
- Harveys Steamed Oyster Saloon. Corner C & [?] St.
- Gurner, Wm. Oyster Saloon. Corner C &1st Sts.

- Sullivan, P. Baltimore & Washington House. Corner C & 1st Sts. Low class.
- Spalding, Jas. Columbia House. C St. below 1st St. Low class.
- Hamilton, Chas. R. Lager Beer Restaurant. C St. 2nd door below 1st St. Low class.
- Mearus & Duffie. Union House. Corner C St. & N.Y. Ave. Low class.
- Bennett, C.W. Harbour Restaurant. 283 C St. 2nd class.
- Luts, A. Luts Hotel. Corner C & 10th Sts. 3rd class.
- Leary, Ellen. Rum Mill. Corner C & 11th Sts. Low class.
- Heifer, Philip. Lager Beer Saloon. Corner C & 10th Sts. Low class.
- Flannigan, James. Grocery & Liquors. Corner C & 10th Sts. Low class.
- Whalom, Wm. Grocery & Liquors. Corner C & 2nd Sts. Island. Low class.
- Brady, Peter. Grocery & Liquors. Corner C & 2nd Sts. Island. Low class.
- Gerheirt, J. Germany Hotel. 346 C St. 3rd class.
- McNichol, T. Mrs. Exchange Hotel. 358 C St. 3rd class.
- Hemrick, L. New York Hotel. 360 C St. 3rd class.

COMMERCE ON LETTERED STREETS

- Colerm, Jas. Kimmell Restaurant. (Basement) 357 C St. 4th class.
- Kimmell. Kimmell House & Stage Office. 359 & 357 C St. 2nd class.
- Boyle, C. Depot House. C St. between N.Y. Ave. & 1st St. 3rd class.
- Watson, J. (Colored) Drinking House. 13th & C Sts. Low class.
- Hersch, A. Grocery & Liquors. 13th & C Sts.

D STREET

- Brian, Michael. Grocery & Liquors. Corner D & 14th Sts. Fair.
- Sputsvisits Restaurant & Bawdy House. 313 D. St. Very low.
- O'Connell, D. Restaurant. Corner D & 13th Sts. 3rd class.
- Roberts, M.F. Restaurant. 315 D St. 4th class.
- Higles, Jacob. Restaurant. 319 D St. 3rd class.
- Schwinghammer, E. Grocery &Liquors. Corner of D & 13 ½ Sts.
- Donnelly, Peter. Grocery & Liquors. Corner of D & 13 ½ Sts.
- McCafferty, Hugh. Grocery & Liquors (Island) D & 2nd Sts. 4th class.

- Rosenthall, J. Winter Garden Concert & Saloon. 318 D St. 2nd class.
- Hoch, Augustus. Military Hall. 340 D St. 3rd class.
- Dengall & Co. Restaurant (Basement) Corner D & 9th Sts. 3rd class.
- Martin, Cyras. Franklin House. Corner of D & 8th Sts. 3rd class.
- Brandner, F. Richmond House. Corner D & 8th Sts. 3rd class.
- Rainey, R. Hotel & Drinking Room. D St. near 7th St. 3rd class.
- Metropolitan Hall Concert & Lager Beer Saloon. Hensel, Mensyl, & Merklein, Proprietors. D St. between 12th & 13th Sts. 3rd class. [all one entry.]
- Baygar & Steubener, Restaurant, Union Hotel. D & 13 ½ Sts. 3rd class.

E STREET

- Wicks, Cornelius. Oyster Saloon. Corner E & 6th Sts. (Col) Low class.
- Adams, Marshal. Restaurant. 311 8th & E [?] (Col)
- Rankins Restaurant. 350 E St. at 8th.
- Howell, Daniel. Restaurant. 452 E St. at 8th.
- Martin, Fred. Lager Beer Saloon. 124 East Capitol St. 4th class.

- Mitchell, Jas. Military Shade [sic]. 19 East Capitol St. Low class.

- Peter Viersbuchen. Wm. Tell House. 5 East Capitol St. Low class.

- [No name listed]. Oyster Saloon. 319 E St.

- Pennington, Mrs. (Col'd.) Porter & Ale Saloon. 322 18th St. between H & L.

- Burrick, Jas. Porter & Ale Saloon. 18th St. between L & [?].

- Palmer, Martha. 315 18th St. between H & L.

- Baygar & Steuben. Union Hotel. Corner 13 ½ & E Sts.

- Grembusch, A. White Beer Brewery. 509 11th St. Fair [class]

- Hendrick & Trinder. Cosmopolitan House. 525 11th St. 4th class.

- Haebiels, Chas. Lager Beer & Liquor Saloon. Corner E & 11th Sts. Low.

- McGee, Wm. C. Bowling & Drinking Saloon. 325 E St. Low.

- Lander House. Restaurant. 362 11th St.

- Emrick, P. European Hotel. Corner 11th St. & Pa. Ave. 3rd class.

- Ontrick & Bryan. Theatre Restaurant. 507 E St. & 11th St. 3rd class.

- McKenzie, Peter. Grocery & Liquor Store. Cor. E & 20th Sts. Low, disorderly.
- Callahan, Patrick. Grocery & Liquor Store. Corner E & 20th Sts. Low.
- Goetz, E. Hotel. Corner E & 10th Sts. 3rd class.
- Tillman, Louis. Hotel. Corner E & 11th Sts. 3rd class.
- Braggoth, Jas. Hotel. 362 E St. between 11th & 12th Sts. 3rd class.
- Johnson, Wm. Restaurant. 510 [?] 11th St.
- Brown, Francis (Col'd). Porter & Ale. 513 11th St.
- Hartforth, August. Hotel. Corner of E & 4 ½ Sts. (Island). 4th class.
- Haldzes [?], Fred. Restaurant. 3rd St, east of Capitol. 4th class.
- Campbells Saloon. 298 E St. 2nd class.
- Usher, John. White House Restaurant. 312 E St. 2nd class.
- Barber, Pat (Col'd). Saratoga Saloon. 318 E St. 4th class.
- Carrigan, John. Metropolitan Saloon. 328 E St. 2nd class.
- Rankin & Rich. New York Restaurant. 330 E St. 3rd class.
- Mitchels Restaurant. 332 E St. 1st class.
- West, J.D. Delphie House. 328 E St. 3rd class.

- Kelly, Michael. Restaurant (Negro resort). 330 E St. Low class.
- Tultz, Stephen. Restaurant (Negro resort). 332 E St. Low class.
- Hogan, Mrs. National Restaurant (Negro resort). 334 E St. Low class.
- Gleason, Wm. Gleason House. Corner E & 13th Sts. 3rd class.
- Gibson, J. Post Office Restaurant. Corner E & 7th Sts. 3rd class.
- Green, W.L. Restaurant. Corner E & 8th Sts. 3rd class.
- Shields, Catharine. Grocery & Liquors. E St. between 14th & 15th Sts. 3rd class.

F STREET

(This section of the provost marshal's records, marked page 134 in a large ledger, is clearly and legibly marked "Hotels & & & [sic] on F Street," yet the first nine entries make no mention of F Street.)

- Fletcher, John. Restaurant. 605 4th St.
- McLaughlin, D. Grocery & Liquor Store. 4th & I Sts.
- Scollin, D. Grocery & Liquor Store. 4th & K Sts.
- Chas. Pearson. Grocery & Liquor Store. 225 4th St.
- O'Brien, F. Grocery & Liquor Store. 189 4th St.
- Coton, John. Grocery & Liquor Store. 393 5th St.

- Brian Nathan. Grocery & Liquor Store. 14th St. between Ohio Ave. & D St.
- Herman, P. Restaurant. 196 14th St. between D & E Sts. 4th class.
- Butler's Restaurant. 406 14th St. 2nd class.
- Birch, C.J. Billiard Saloon. Between Pa. Ave. & F St. 14th St. (sic)
- Dougherty, C. H. Grocery & Liquor. 406 14th St.
- Rowels, Jas. Grocery & Liquor. 14th St. between O & P Sts. (sic).
- Ray, N.B. Grocery & Liquor. 14th St. between O & P Sts. (sic).
- Maimies, R.S. Hotel. 14th St. between O & P Sts.
- Townett, F. Lager Beer Saloon. 146 14th St.
- Forsson, August. Restaurant & Liquor. 14th St. between O & P Sts. Disorderly.
- Marshal, E.A. Grocery & Liquor. 15th St. between L & M Sts. Disorderly.
- Leary, O.D. Grocery & Liquor. 14th St. between L & M Sts.
- Guilds, James. Grocery & Liquor. Corner F & 2nd Sts.
- Brooks & Phillips. Grocery & Liquor. 25 4 ½ St.
- Murphy Misses. Porter & Ale. Corner 5th & F Sts.
- Jeremiah Costell. Grocery & Liquor. 332 4th St.
- Downeys. Grocery & Liquor. 305 4th St.
- John C. Caton. Grocery & Liquor. 533 4th St.

- Patterson, Mrs. Mary. Grocery & Liquor. 86 4 ½ St. Island.
- Brent, Geo. Steamed Oyster Saloon. 248 F St. Island.
- Jones. Rum Mill. Corner F & 20th Sts. Very low.
- Murphy, John. Rum Mill. F St. one door from 20th St. Very low.
- Craney, A.H. Ebbett House. 233,235, and 237 F St. 1st class.
- Land, Jas. (Col'd.) St. Nichols Restaurant. 405 F St. 4th class.
- Kennedy, John. Rum Mill. F St. 2nd door from 20th St. Very low.
- Bryan, Geo. Rum Mill. F St. 3rd door from 20th St. Very low.
- Taylor, John. Rum Mill & Bawdy house. F St. 4th door from 20th St. Very low.
- Brady, John. Rum Mill. F St. 5th door from 20th St. Very low.
- Finnegan, Annie. Rum Mill & Bawdy House. F St. 6th door from 20th St. Very low.
- Coway, Ed. Rum Mill. F St. 7th door from 20th St. Very low.
- Biggins, Thos. Rum Mill. F St. 9th door from 20th St. Very low.
- Cummiskey, John. Rum Mill. No. 125 (sic) F St. 10th door from 20th St. Very low.

- Jackson & White. Rum Mill. F St. 11th door from 20th St. Very low.
- Scherger, M. Restaurant. Corner F St. & 12th St. 3rd class.
- Flannigan, Jas. Restaurant. 195 F St. 4th class.
- DeLacey, Richard. Bar room. 193 F St. 3rd class.
- Riley, Thomas. Rum Mill. Corner 5th & 21st. (sic) Low class.
- Burns, Thomas. Rum Mill. 14th St. between D St. & Ohio Ave.
- Kelly, John. Grocery & Liquor. 4 ½ St. between [?] & C Sts.
- McGuire, Pat. Grocery & Liquor. 252 F St. between 1st & 2nd Sts. Island.
- Tepper, Mathew. Grocery & Liquor. 180 4 ½ St. Island. 4th class.
- Gibbens, Pat. Rum Mill. 68 4 ½ St. Island. Low class.
- Kelly, Pat. Rum Mill. 66 4 ½ St. Island. Low class.
- Keenan, J. Grocery & Liquor. 202 4th St. Island. Low class.
- Thompson, Robert. Grocery & Liquor. Corner F & 4 ½ Sts. Island. 4th class.
- Donley, Richard. Grocery & Liquor. Corner F & 4 ½ Sts. Island. 4th class.
- Bergdorf, A. Restaurant. 389 4 ½ St. Island. 3rd class.

- Thompson, Frank. Treasury Restaurant. 476 15th St. 4th class.
- Bailor, Capt. Restaurant. 214 F St. 4th class.
- Smith & Pettet. Grocery & Liquor. 11th & F Sts. 4th class.
- Murray, T.J. Herndon House. Corner F & 9th Sts. 3rd class.
- Hipps, S.M. Model House. Corner F & 9th Sts. 3rd class.

G STREET

- Lord, William. Grocery & Liquor Store. Corner G & 5th Sts.
- McMann, James. Saloon. Corner G & 20th Sts.
- Kaegle [?], Owen. Restaurant & Liquor. Corner 20th & G Sts. Low class.
- Heeling, Wm. J. Restaurant. Corner G & 22nd Sts. 3rd class.
- Gale, A. Restaurant. 141 G St. between 21st & 22nd. Low class.
- Conley, James. Restaurant. 158 G St. between 21st & 22nd Sts. Low class.
- Clark, John [?]. Restaurant. Corner G & 17th Sts. 3rd class.
- Riley, John. Saloon. Corner G & 18th Sts. 3rd class.

- Klatz, Chas. Restaurant. 237 G St. 3rd class.
- Creed, Jeremiah. Bar room. 210 G St. Low class.
- Bangermel, A. Saloon. 231 G St. 3rd class.
- Reynolds, J.W. McClellan House. 208 G St. 3rd class.
- Peacock, Geo. Restaurant. 237 G St. between 21st & 22nd Sts.
- Gaynor, John. Rum Mill. Corner G St. & 21st St. Low class.
- Costello, Jeremiah. Grocery & Liquor. Corner G St. & 4th St. Low class.
- Webb, N.T. Restaurant. 403 G St. 3rd Class.

H STREET

- Wagoner, Chas. Grocery & Liquor Store. Corner H & 5th Sts.
- Hays, Bernard. Grocery & Liquor Store. Corner H & 4th Sts.
- McCarty, Chas. Grocery & Liquor Store. Corner H & 18th Sts.
- Cogan, Thos. Grocery & Liquor Store. Corner H & 20th Sts. Fair class.
- Bradley, Wm. Russell House. 191 H St. between 18th & 19th Sts. 2nd class.
- Menney, J. Rum Mill. Corner H & 22nd Sts. Low class.

- Robert Middleton. Restaurant. Corner H & East Capitol Sts.
- Harvey, J.M. St[eamed] Oyster Saloon. 189 H. St. 2nd class.
- Conner, J. Grocery & Liquor. Corner 6th & H Sts. 3rd class.
- Henelly, M. Grocery & Liquor. Corner H & 2nd St. 3rd class.
- Grogens, Thos. Restaurant. 3rd & H Sts. 4th class.

I ("Eye") STREET

- Hagman, Louis. Grocery, Porter, & Ale. Corner I & 9th Sts.
- Berth, Wm. Grocery & Liquor. Corner Ind. Ave. & 3rd St.
- Jefferson, B.W. Grocery & Liquor. Corner Ind. Ave. & 3rd St.
- Frazier, John. Grocery & Liquor. Corner I & 18th Sts.
- Murray, John. Restaurant. 195 I St. between 19th & 20$^{th.}$ Sts. 4th class.
- Pfifer, John C. Restaurant. 167 I St. between 21st & 22nd Sts. 4th class.
- Williams, John. Restaurant. 229 I St. between 21st and 22nd Sts. 4th class.

- Beam, Jas. Restaurant. Corner I & 11th Sts. East Capitol. 3rd class.
- Masceron, M. Restaurant. [No address recorded.]
- Mayher, Jas. Grocery & Liquor. Corner I & 4 ½ Sts. Island. 4th class.
- Howard & Hendy. Restaurant. Ind. Ave. between 1st & 2nd Sts. 3rd class.
- Morgan, Geo. Beer & Ale. I St. between 12th & 13th Sts. 3rd class.
- Jeire F. & Co. Grocery & Liquor. Corner I & 6th Sts. 3rd class.

J STREET

There was no J street. In the 18th and 19th centuries, a capital "I" and a capital "J" looked the same. In the army, regiments were numbered and companies bore letters. There were never a "Company J." It is obvious that the intent, in both street naming and in unit designation, was to prevent confusion.

K STREET

- Murray, Jas. Rum Mill. Corner K & 20th Sts.
- Kelly, Jas. Grocery & Liquor. Corner K & 4 ½ Sts. Island. 4th class.

- McKeever, Thos. Wine & Liquors. Corner K St. between 19th & 20th Sts. 3rd class.
- Erb & Milkerson. Restaurant. 234 K St. 3rd class.
- Scanlon, E.D. Grocery & Liquor. Corner K & 4th Sts. Low class.

L STREET

- Wilson, Patrick. Grocery, Porter, & Ale. Corner L & 4th Sts.
- Hughes, John. Grocery & Liquor. Corner L & 19th Sts.
- Gleason, Tim. Restaurant. Corner L & 20th Sts.
- Tynan, John. Rum Mill. Corner L & 16th Sts.
- Kelly, Mrs. Grocery & Liquor. Corner L & 16th Sts.
- Ervin, Dennis. Grocery & Liquor. Corner L & 8th Sts.
- Mehrlins, Philip. Restaurant. Corner Louisiana Ave. & 9th St. 3rd class.
- Riley, Peter. Grocery & Liquor. 399 L St. between 4th & 5th Sts. Low class.
- Holland, Mrs. M.A. Grocery & Liquor. L St. between 1st & 2nd Sts. Low class.
- Hagin, Mrs. Grocery & Liquor. 218 L St. Low class.
- Richardson, J. Oyster Saloon. Corner 13th & L Sts. 2nd class.

M STREET

This appears to include any street or avenue that begins with the letter "M," such as M Street, Massachusetts, Maine, and Maryland Avenues.

- Feeney, Cornelius. Liquor Shop. Corner Mass. Ave. & 3rd St.

- Crogar, Thomas. Restaurant. Corner Mass. Ave. & 3rd St.

- Rhoads, Mrs. J. Drinking & Bawdy House. 474 Md. Ave. Low class.

- Erbaze, Chas. Lager Beer Brewery. 330 Md. Ave.

- Mills, Mrs. M. Grocery & Liquor Store. Md. Ave. & 4th St.

- Green, James. Grocery & Liquor Store. Corner M & 20th Sts.

- Harrell, George. Grocery & Liquor Store. Corner M & 20th Sts.

- Losburg, M. Porter & Ale. Corner M & 18th Sts. Low class.

- Shanahan, Jno. Union Tavern. Mass. Ave. & 12th St.

- Jackson, Mrs. H. Restaurant. Corner Maine Ave. & 4 ½ St. Low class.

- Beck, John. Mechanics Hall & Ballroom. 398 Md. Ave. Island. 3rd class.

- Thompson, Benjamin. Grocery & Liquor. Corner Md. Ave. & 4 ½ St. Island. 4th cl.

COMMERCE ON LETTERED STREETS

- Amour, Mrs. D. Grocery & Liquor. Corner M & 22nd St. 4th class.
- Redman, J. Grocery & Liquor. 434 Mass. Ave.

N STREET

- Daley, Patrick. Grocery & Liquor. Corner N.Y. Ave. & 4th St.
- Kiod [?], Jacob. Grocery & Liquor. Corner N & 5th Sts.
- Gass & Gotley. Lager Beer Restaurant. 389 9th St.
- Hanf, Louis. Lager Beer Restaurant. 400 9th St.
- Surgo, F.H. Restaurant. 507 9th St.
- Burch, J.W. Restaurant. 527 9th St. 3rd class.
- Nephuth, Philip. Restaurant. 531 9th St.
- Davis, J.W. Grocery & Liquor. Corner 9th & E Sts.
- Morgan, Patrick. Restaurant. 508 N.J. Ave. below C St.
- Muntz, John. Restaurant & Bawdy House. 512 N.J. Ave.
- Lester & Co. Connecticut House. 510 N.J. Ave.
- O'Leary's Green House Restaurant. 514 N.J. Ave.
- Ritner [?], John. New York Restaurant. 516-518 N.J. Ave.
- Kelly, M. Railroad House. 520 N.J. Ave. Low class.
- Tepper, M. Turner Hall. 522 N.J. Ave.

- Donaldson, Geo. White House Restaurant. 528 N.J. Ave.
- Birch, C.J. [Rest of entry blank]
- White & Noff. Porter & Ale. Corner N St. & Conn. Ave. Low class.
- Ruple, Jacob. Restaurant & Liquor. 369 19th St. 3rd class.
- Willer [?], Chas. Drinking saloon. N St. between 4 ½ & 6th Sts. Island. 3rd class.
- Miller, John. Restaurant & Hotel. Corner N & 6th Sts. Island. 3rd class.
- Wait, Mrs. Potomac House. Corner N & 6th Sts. 4th class.
- Stafford, John. Grocery & Liquor. Corner N & 4 ½ Sts. 4th class.
- Marcks, Wm. Lager beer saloon. Corner N & 4 ½ Sts. Island. 4th class.
- Clorian, T.H. Oyster saloon. N.Y. Ave. between 14th & 15th Sts. 4th class.
- Dilli, George. Market Restaurant. Corner N.Y. Ave. & 7th St. 3rd class.
- Dailey, Pat. Grocery & Liquor. Corner N.Y. Ave. & 4th St. Low class.
- Lepierre [?], E. Restaurant & Lager Beer Saloon. Corner N.Y. Ave. between 1st & 2nd Sts. 3rd class.

O STREET

- Bellens, Thos. Grocery & Liquor. Corner O & 9th Sts.
- Brian Thomas. Grocery & Liquor. Corner Ohio Ave. & 14th St.
- Hosch, August. Grocery & Liquor. Corner Ohio Ave. & 13 ½ St.

P, Q, and R STREETS

The available records do not contain entries for these three streets.

S STREET

- Conoughlan, Dennis. Grocery & Liquor. 19 6th St.
- McMahon & Refer. Oyster Saloon. 2nd St. between Pa. Ave. & B St.
- Grogan & Bush. Restaurant. 446 6th St.
- Thomas, M.M. Billiard Saloon. 497 6th St.
- Dubrants Eating Saloon. 499 6th St.
- Gallagher, J. Restaurant. 489 6th St.
- Lurch, Henry G. Armory Hall. Island. 572 7th St. 4th class.
- Dixon, Chas. Grocery & Liquor. 6th St. & Ind. Ave. Low class.

- Thomas, John. Restaurant & Liquor Store. 669 7th St. between E & F Sts.
- Venderlick, John. Restaurant. 619 7th St. between H & L Sts. E. Capitol. Low.
- Frank, Jas. Porter & Ale Shop.17th St. between L & N. Low class.
- Laskey, Wm. Restaurant. 7th St. between Pa. Ave. & B St. 3rd class.
- Shackelford, Wm. [Remainder of entry is blank.]
- Cool & Johnson. Restaurant. 556 7th St. Wst. (sic) 2nd class.
- Richter & Schonborn. Restaurant & Lager Beer Saloon. 552 7th St. Wst. 3rd class.
- Kraventler, Adolph. Restaurant & Lager Beer Saloon. 534 7th St. Wst. 3rd class.
- Roby, Andrew J. Hotel. 556 7th St. Wst. 2nd class.
- Pumphries, Jas. Restaurant. 586 7th St. Island. 4th class.
- Andrews, Wm. Restaurant. 648 7th St. between L & M. 4th class.
- Murtsgary's Rum Mill. Corner 20th & F Sts. Low class.
- Kloman, Chas. Restaurant & Saloon. 509 7th St.
- Dilly, George. Restaurant & Saloon. 336 7th St.

T STREET

Once again, a mystery. This page in the provost ledger book, page 160, is clearly headed "T Street," yet there is hardly any mention of that street. As an example, Bell's Steamed Oyster Saloon is listed at "493 10th Street." Was that near an intersection with T Street? If so, a clerk 150 years ago left us no clue. These establishment are presented just as they were written, without second-guessing any intent.

- Horscher, A. Grocery & Liquor. 13 ½ St. [sic]
- Murphy, [?]. Grocery & Liquor. 415 3rd St.
- Foster, Thos. Eating Saloon (Col'd). 3rd St. between Pa. Ave. & C. Low class.
- Dunn, Mrs. Union House. 288 3rd St. Low class.
- Clemmens, A. Steamed Oyster Saloon. 330 12th St.
- Bell, J.W. & Co. Steamed Oyster Saloon. 493 10th St.
- Giffon, Amos. Restaurant. 262 20th St.
- Hays, Thomas. Porter & Ale Saloon. 202 20th St.
- Haggerty, Pat. Porter & Ale Saloon. 213 20th St.
- [No owner named]. Grocery & Liquor. 20th St. between M & N.
- Myers, Wm. Restaurant. 22nd St. between G & H.
- Larlinger, Jos. Wm. Tell Hall. 429 13th St. between D & E. 4th class.
- Nathens, Joseph. Ceder [?] Assembly Room. 12th St. between C & B.
- MacEntire, Mrs. Porter & Ale Shop. 332 12th St.

- Lynander, Jn. Thiels[?] House Restaurant. 439 13th St.
- Goodman, Thos. Potomac Restaurant. 440 20th St. Low class.
- Thompson, Mary. Grocery & Liquor. 133 21st St. between G & H.
- B [no other identification]. Grocery & Liquor. 116 23rd St. Very low class.
- Weibel, Julian. Restaurant. 487 10th St. between D & C.
- Shakelfer, Wm. Green Room [?] Saloon. 454 10th St. between D & C.
- O'Flannagan, K. Hotel. 550 12th St. Low class.
- Lockwell, M. Headquarters. Bawdy House & Restaurant. 552 12th St. 4th class.
- Carbessy, John. Rum Mill. 499 3rd St. between Md. Ave. & B. Low class.
- Halzer, Fred. Restaurant. 3rd St. east of Capitol. 4th class.
- Mitchell & Kirby. Kirby House. 462, 464, & 466 13th St. 2nd class.
- Rothery, B. Oyster & Drinking Saloon. 24th St. between Pa. Ave. & L. Low class.
- French, R. Grocery & Liquor. 24th St. between H & I Sts. 4th class.

- O'Day, Ann. Grocery & Liquor. 25th St. between I & H Sts. Low class.
- Barrett, Michael. Grocery & Liquor. 94 26th St.
- Morgan, Mary. Grocery & Liquor. 26th St. between G & H Sts. Low class.
- McLaughlin, Pat. Grocery & Liquor. 26th St. between F & G Sts. Fair class.
- Haden, Mrs. Grocery & Liquor. 26th St. corner of H. Fair class.

CHAPTER 4
PATTERNS

Our major data comes from two lists. First is that of the establishments along Pennsylvania Avenue; the second list shows all the other establishments, both north and south of Pennsylvania Avenue. The two groups reflect very different patterns of commerce, especially commerce of interest to a tourist, whether soldier or citizen.

The compilers of the lists did not use uniform terminology. The lists give quality ratings to some businesses and not to others. Many business have a name, but no indication of the commerce pursued therein. Examples are Kirkwood House, Washington House, Capitol House, Arlington House, Delevan House, and Simpson House. This lack of uniformity leads to some confusion as to exact percentages, but general trends are readily visible.

Along Pennsylvania Avenue we see this distribution:

Type of Business	Number
Restaurant	23
Hotel	15
Saloon	4
Lager Beer Saloon	3
Oyster Saloon	3
Grocery & Liquor	1

In contrast with Pennsylvania Avenue, the other areas in the District of Columbia reflect a different trade, with a prevalence of lower class eating places and liquor stores. The term "Grocery & Liquor" is common, but the visiting soldiers were usually fed in camp and had no means of cooking while visiting the city. Most likely the "grocery" was the Civil War equivalent of snack foods and "liquor" dominated sales. Here is the distribution of establishments *not* on Pennsylvania.

Type of Business	Number
Restaurant	89
Grocery & Liquor	84
Rum Mill	22
Hotel	14
Oyster Saloon	12
Saloon	12
Porter & Ale	10
Billiard Saloon	1

In the non-Pennsylvania Ave areas the provost marshal compiler gave ratings to nearly half of the establishments. The distribution trend is hard to miss. The soldier who wandered north or south of the main avenue was not in four-star Michelin territory. Here are the categories and the number in each category

First class	2
Second class	13
Third class	55
Fourth class	36
Low class	47
Very low class	13

A further breach in uniform data collection were six businesses away from Pennsylvania Avenue that combined liquor, food, and sex. They will be listed here and appear again in the compilations of bordellos.

- Sputsvisits Restaurant & Bawdy House. 313 D St. Very low class.
- Taylor, John. Rum Mill & Bawdy House. F St. near 20th. Very low class.
- Finnegan, Annie. Rum Mill & Bawdy House. F St. near 20th. Very low class.
- Rhoads, Mrs. J. Drinking & Bawdy House. 474 Md. Ave. Low class.
- Muntz, John. Restaurant & Bawdy House. 512 N. J. Ave. [Not rated].
- Lockwell, M. "Headquarters" Bawdy House & Restaurant. 552 12th St. 4th class.

It does not require the sophistication of today's Global Information Systems to see the trend in Civil War District of Columbia: the farther from Pennsylvania Avenue the deeper the descent into low class debauchery.

CHAPTER 5
GAMBLING

Frank Sinatra sang, "Luck be a Lady Tonight." In ancient Rome, the hope was far more formal: they worshipped an actual deity, the Goddess Fortuna, whose temples have been found all around Rome. But gambling goes back much further. Six thousand years ago in ancient Mesopotamia, knucklebones were used as dice. Five thousand years ago, the Egyptians were playing the ancestor of backgammon. Between the Romans and the American Civil War gambling continued to flourish. Gambling always involves wishful thinking, the feeling that, "Just for me, at this very moment, the odds, the actual statistics, will be mystically shifted in my favor." A satirical poem *Das Narrenschiff* (Ship of Fools), published in 1494, skewered many human failings, included gambling.

Faro (also known as Faro Bank) was played as early as 1600 A.D. It was the rage across the Old West and every saloon had a game in progress. Faro was popular with the players because the rules were simple.

It was an absolute boon to the men running the game because cheating was so easy; in fact, supply houses sold cheating equipment. A history published by the Bicycle Playing Card Company claims that during the Civil War there were 150 faro games running in Washington, DC. (Sadly, the article gives no source.)

We do, however, have better documentation of faro in the courts-martial of four Union men. Lieut. Col. A. L. Thomas, US Volunteers, lost $1,700 of government money playing faro in Washington, DC. (That's about $50,000 in today's money.) Lieut. Col. A. von Steinhauser, 138th US Colored Troops, played faro at Long Island, Alabama, and at Shellmound, Tennessee. First Lieut. E. H. Mace, 1st US Infantry, while on patrol in New Orleans, left his men on the street and went indoors to play faro. Capt. Walter Johnson, US Coast Guard, kept prostitute Anna Morley in his quarters at Fort Monroe, Virginia. He also cheated his sergeant out of $30 by playing faro.

Chuck-a-luck was also quite popular. Let us consider the court-martialed officers first. Capt. John J. Fowler, 12th Iowa, gambled at chuck-a-luck at Corinth, Mississippi. Capt. Joseph Parke, 4th Missouri Militia Cavalry, gambled at chuck-a-luck with enlisted men, at Tipton, Missouri. Capt. George W. Stobie, 28th Illinois, gambled at chuck-a-luck with enlisted men, at White's

Station, Tennessee. Capt. James Boultinghouse, 34th Kentucky, gambled at chuck-a-luck at Cumberland Gap, Tennessee. (He was also tried for bad language about President Lincoln.)

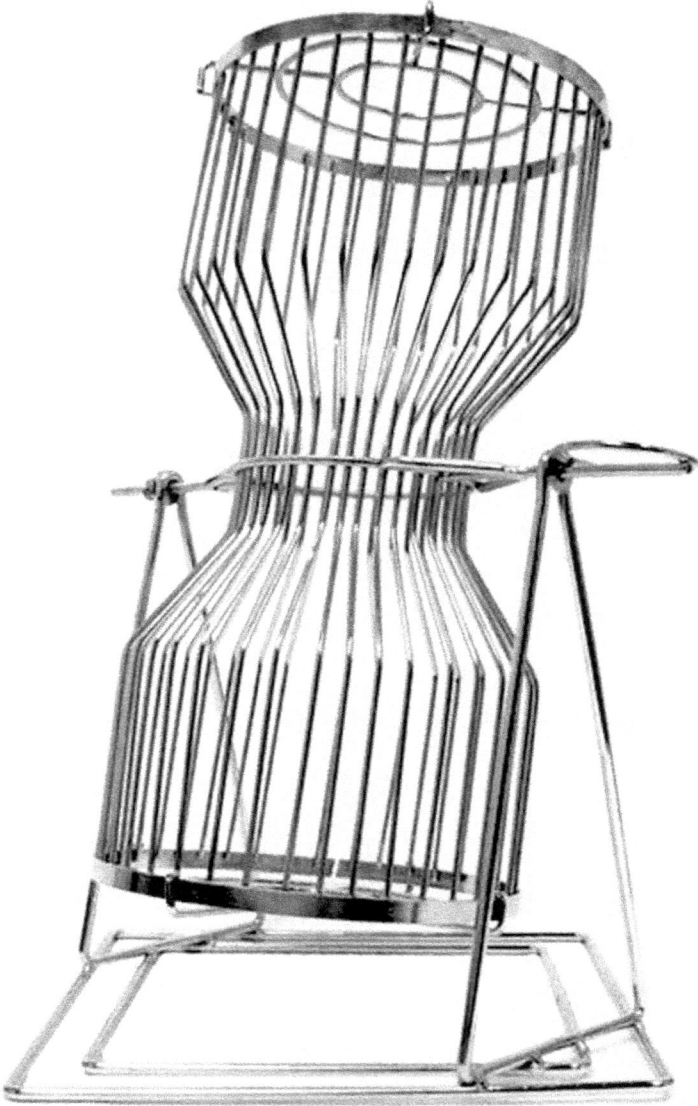

Pvt. Thomas Stateler, 4th Missouri Militia Cavalry, ran a chuck-a-luck bank. Pvt. William Thompson, 91st Indiana, ran a chuck-a-luck game at Madisonville, Kentucky, and won $64 from another private. Pvt. Frank Short, 14th Ohio, gambled at chuck-a-luck at LaVergne, Tennessee. Corp. George Ringo, 13th Kansas, gambled at chuck-a-luck with enlisted men at Little Rock, Arkansas. Pvts. Otto Derringer and John Collins gambled at chuck-a-luck with colored enlisted men. Pvt. Z. H. Evans, 12th Kansas, also gambled at chuck-a-luck with colored enlisted men.

There were twenty-four other courts-martial related to gambling in the Union army, presented here in order of rank. Col. John McCluskey, 15th Maine, on the transport ship *Great Republic*, cursed a captain who had criticized men for gambling. Col. John M. Comparet, 142nd Indiana, failed to arrest professional gamblers at Nashville, Tennessee. Major William B. Olmsted, 5th New York Excelsior Brigade, among five other offenses, released two prisoners arrested for gambling. Major Thomas H. Penney, 33rd Missouri, not only stole horses and chickens, but on the steamboat *John Bell* stayed up all night drinking and gambling.

Capt. Amos A. Rouse, 5th Michigan Veteran Volunteers, cheated enlisted men using a "swet board" and crooked dice. Capt. William Rhode, 58th Ohio, took a bribe to protect a gambling house at Vicksburg, Mississippi. Capt. Adam T. Ault, 22nd Iowa, gambled with enlisted men. Capt. Henry S. Lucas, 12th Pennsylvania, encouraged gambling at Chantilly, Virginia.

First Lieut. William H. Carpenter, 34th Ohio, plied a citizen with government whiskey and won money from him at cards. First Lieut. William H. Harris, 89th New York, stayed in his tent gambling for money at Folly Island, South Carolina, during an attack. Second Lieut. Timothy F. Lee, 9th Massachusetts, played cards with enlisted men at Fort Corcoran, Virginia, winning $60. Second Lieut. Charles S. Smith, 11th Vermont, gambled with enlisted men and with a servant, and denied it. Second Lieut. Isham Reed, 70th Indiana, was drunk and gambling with enlisted men at Savannah, Georgia. Second Lieut. Andrew Hill, 1st Missouri Light Artillery, gambled at billiards and the "Pigion Hole Game," at New Orleans. Lieut. J. S. Dunning, 7th Connecticut, used marked cards to cheat sergeants at Tybee Island, Georgia.

Pvt. William Bancroft, 86th US Colored Troops, would not work, played cards and gambled instead, at Barrancas, Florida. Pvt. Frank Shock, 8th Veterans Reserve, lay about the saloons of Chicago, drinking and gambling. Pvt. Patrick Rafferty, 66th New York, gambled on picket at Morrisville. He also called his major a "goddamned son of a bitch" and tried to bayonet him. Pvt. Trinidad Rodrigues, Vidal's Texas Cavalry, shot and killed a private at Brownsville, Texas, over a gambling debt. Pvt. Moses Conklin, 8th Indiana, drunkenly pointed a loaded revolver at his sergeant at a Memphis, Tennessee gambling house. Pvt. Timothy W. Keefe, 108th New York, struck his captain and refused to stop gambling. Citizen Benjamin Johnson ran a gambling house full of thieves at Lawrence, Kansas. Citizen Henry H. Leopold had soldiers gambling at his room at Algiers, Louisiana. In the final days of the war, the Confederacy burned their own capital, destroying millions of records. This may explain why we found only one gambling Confederate, Second Lieut. H. Shaw, 10th South Carolina, who gambled with enlisted men.

There is certainly adequate documentation that military gambling was found in every corner of the country. What about Washington, DC? What would a soldier or a tourist find if he wished to try his luck in the Federal capital? The provost marshal's records reveal thirteen recognized gambling houses:

- Sharp & Finegan. 240 Pa. Ave.
- Anthony Ficker. E St., first door below 13th St.
- Joseph Hall. 314 E St.
- John Kelly. 308 E St.

- Andrew McKee. 302 E St.
- A. D. Hayden. 298 E St.
- Hammack's. 202 Pa. Ave.
- Thompkins & Harkins. 231 Pa. Ave.
- Edward Price. 225 Pa. Ave.
- J. Housewright. 468 14th St.
- W. Wilkinson. 406 Pa. Ave.
- A. Bennett. 402 Pa. Ave.
- H. Farris. 400 Pa. Ave.

The distribution of the Washington, DC gambling houses is remarkable. There are seven in only three blocks of the city's most prestigious avenue. They were no secret. Did they cater to those with more money, such as officers and contractors? And why were five houses within a block of each other on E Street? Did E Street cater to another group, perhaps to enlisted men whose pockets had less cash?

The answers to these questions and many more lie in the largely unused records in the National Archives, records of crime, treason, and subversion. Those who wish to extend their Civil War interests beyond one more rehash of Gettysburg will find their guide in the Appendix.

CHAPTER 6

THE PLEDGE

R.H.I.P. "Rank Hath its Privileges." At most posts
the officer's club is more elegant that the NCO (non-
commissioned officers) club, which in turn is more elegant than the facility for enlisted men. An enlisted man
salutes. The officer returns the salute. In the Civil War
courts-martial records, there are many cases involving
drinking in a tent. The enlisted drinkers are arrested or
deprived of their alcohol. The officers who are con-
fronted about drinking in the tents become quite in-
dignant, and claim that as "gentlemen" they are
entitled to their wine and whiskey. These same issues

are seen in a remarkable document from the Washington DC provost marshal's files. It is headed by this paragraph.

"We the undersigned licensed of and by the corporation of the City of Washington to sell spirituous liquors wines and ales. In consideration of the modification by the Provost Marshal of this city of the restrictions and regulations now in force regulating the sale of the same do hereby severally promise and pledge ourselves, not to sell or give or permit to be sold or given on our premises any liquor, either spirituous or malt, to any volunteer or enlisted man or to any person wearing the uniform of a volunteer or enlisted man of the army of the United States or employee in the quarter master department, and that we will strictly comply with the ordinance in regard to the sale of liquors on Sunday.

And we severally make this pledge with the full understanding and consent that in case of any infraction or violation of it on our part, individually or otherwise, that our liquors, wines, and ales be seized and confiscated our licenses forfeited and not to be renewed during the existing rebellion."

Two hundred and two proprietors signed a single long document promising to abide by the rules written above. This list of signatories has four columns: Name of proprietor; address of place of business; amount paid for business license; and date when the license was issued. A few entries do not give an address; as an example, the Willard Hotel is just "Willards Hotel." The proprietor assumed, correctly, that *everybody* knew the Willard. One other hotel, the Metropolitan, gave only the name, but the other 200 businesses wrote down a street address.

Sadly for our purposes, the proprietor's names are signatures, many of them indecipherable. The license fees varied from a high of $300 ($9,000 in today's dollars) to $65. As to addresses, about eighty percent are readable, and a simple tabulation will tell something of where a soldier could *not* get a drink. Here are the locations recorded on this document. The number in parentheses is the number of drinking establishments on that street or avenue, arranged in descending order.

Pennsylvania Avenue (23)

7th Street (14)

E Street (6)

10th Street (4)

Bridge Street (4)

D Street (4)

H Street (3)

8th Street (3)

9th Street (3)

14th Street (3)

C Street (2)

I Street (2)

F Street (2)

G Street (2)

13th Street (2)

One each on B Street, L Street, N Street, 1st Street, 6th Street, 11th Street, 12th Street, 19th Street, and 20th Street.

Four proprietors signed with an "X." The provost's scribe added this: James Flanigan 511 C St.; Mary Morgan 26th & G Sts.; William Ryan corner of 3rd and L Sts. These are often Irish names. The fourth "X" case has an illegible last name.

Which proprietors violated their pledge? Did they indeed lose their liquors and their licenses? The path to such answers is described in the Appendix.

206

No.	Names	Place of Business	Amt paid	License expires
131	Langley & Farnam	454. 8th St		
132	J W Reynolds	215 H st	80	
133	Timothy & Hurley	cor Green & Bridge		
134	James Loy	433. 13th cor of G	60	
135	William x Ryan	cor of 3d & I st	60	
136	Chas m Colgan	No. 251. Pa. av.	90	
137	Adolph Givenbeiss	No 395. H	70	
138	J B Motley	270 7th st	90	
139	Saml x Medtul	13th bet 10 & 11	90	
140	Philip Kifer	506 14th st	90	
141	Jos: Nathan	Ohio av & 12th	80	
142	John Gaynor	cor 21st & G	80	
143	James McManus	44 U. 20th st	90	
144	John Bligh	Squan 324 cor 13 & B	30	
145	Andrew Lutz	494. 10th cor. G	114	
146	J G Killion	163. I st	90	
147	Ferd Butler	447 14th st	90	
148	P G Murray	F & 9th st		
149	W R Sluyter	Penn av & 6th		
150	Wm Bannin	8th bet 12 & 13	84	
151	John Thomas	119. F st	90	
152	Burton & Rawling and A Hyfurth	No. 1. 7th st	570	
153		4½ & E sts	23 33/100	
154	Moses Samstag	577 10 st		
155	H Herbert	222 - 4½ st		

79

CHAPTER 7

WASHINGTON'S THEATRES

The provost marshal's files had nothing to say about theatre life in Washington DC during the Civil War, but it was a vital part of any tourist experience, was reported in detail by one of Lincoln's secretaries, and figured in at least seventeen courts-martial. Under the heading "Places of Amusement," *Boyd's Directory*, in 1864, listed five theatres: Ford's Theatre; Grover's Theatre; Washington Theatre; Varieties Concert Saloon; and Canterbury Hall. Here is an introduction to each of these.

Ford's Theatre, of course, will be forever remembered as the location of Lincoln's murder by Confederate sympathizer John Wilkes Booth. It was a new enterprise, having opened for business just two years earlier, under proprietor J. T. Ford. After the war the building was used for many purposes, was the site of a disastrous floor collapse, and now, fully restored is operated by the National Park Service.

Grover's Theatre was erected in 1863 on E Street North between 13th and 14th Streets. The proprietor was Leonard Grover. He and Ford had a cordial rivalry, cordial because the surging population made both men prosperous. Grover's theatre, under one name or another, has been in operation since 1835, and has been visited by every American president since Andrew Jackson. It now exists as the National Theatre, at 1321 Pennsylvania Avenue NW. The night Lincoln was assassinated, his young son, Tad, was at Grover's Theatre, attending a performance of *Aladdin and the Wonderful Lamp*. When the terrible news came, kind hands returned Tad to the White House, where longtime doorkeeper Thomas Pendel attempted to comfort him. Tad cried over and over again, "Oh, they've killed papa dead." Pendel put Tad to bed, put his arm around the boy and talked to him until Tad fell asleep.

A vast diversity of talents has appeared on Grover's stage: Edwin Booth, John Wilkes Booth, James Earl Jones, Eartha Kitt, Lily Tomlin, Laurence Olivier, Annie Oakley, George C. Scott, Rex Harrison, Tim Curry, Will Rogers, Jerry Lewis, Rita Moreno, and hundreds more.

Lincoln himself attended sixteen performances at Grover's Theatre: *The Lakes of Killarney*; *The Latest from New York Phil*; *Hamlet*; *Othello*; *The Ticket of Leave-Man*; *The Iron Chest*; *Catherine and Petruchio*; *Brutus*; *The Merchant of Venice*; *Don Caesar de Bazan*; *Hamlet* (a second time); *Richelieu*; *The Fool's Revenge*; *Too Much for Good Nature*; *Richard III*; *Hamlet* (again); and *Leah, the Forsaken*.

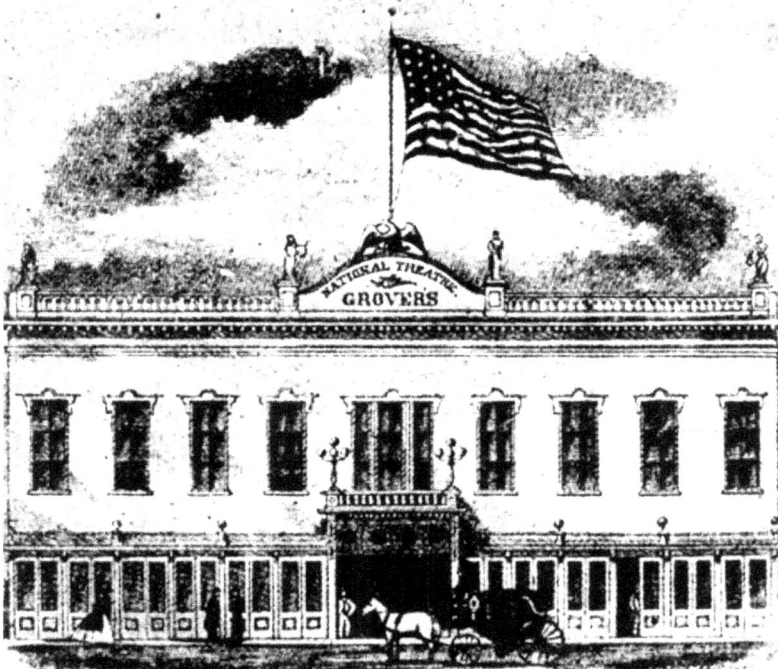

Canterbury Hall, at 32 Louisiana Avenue, was under the guidance of proprietor W. E. Sinn, and seems to have provided somewhat risqué offerings. John Hay, one of Lincoln's two secretaries, kept a very extensive diary, recently re-edited by Michael Burlingame and John R. Turner Ettlinger. The entry for July 5, 1864 gives us a unique glimpse into the Canterbury.

"I went this morning to get places at the Canterbury. I found the lower boxes taken, but they told me at the office that G.C.S. [Green Clay Smith] had taken the one I wanted would probably not occupy it as he generally sat on the stage. I went down to the National to see him about it, was directed to his room & went there alone. Mr. [William C.] Goodloe his nephew opened the door and on my telling what I wanted he asked me into the room where there were 3 Canterbury girls. We had some Bourbon whiskey which the sprightly ladies drank like little men. One of them, overcome by her emotions, retiring for ten minutes or so with Goodloe & then came back to be joked by the envious others.

"I dined with Malet Kennedy & Bob L and went to the Canterbury in the evening. The room was hot and we took off our coats and sat comfortably in the box. Smith's was occupied but I saw him sitting in the flies, fanning the legs of a dancing girl. The show was the Bushwhackers of the Potomac, filthy & not funny except in its burlesque of Beau Hickman [a well-known, rake, gambler, and fancy dresser, noted to be "too proud to work and too honest to steal."] There is a sentinel discovered pacing in front of the Capitol by moonlight. He is quickly shot by the heavy man, the Bushwhacker, who informs the audience that another Yankee has gone to his long home – that he (the B.) has a Union wife & "cherishes a lustful passion" for his sister; both these ladies coming on the stage opportunely he kills the one & requests the other to fly with him – She objects and a miserable hangdog creature comes to the scene in the garb of a lieutenant who of course points his finger in defiance at the bushwhacker who sneaks off saying he will have revenge. We then have a haunted hut & an apparition of Washington – a flash ball – an indecent scene in which some African gypsies strip Beau Hickman's trousers from him – a few bloody fights & a final apotheosis of everybody who has been killed in the play, while the bloody Bushwhacker of course dies miserably." [© SIU Press, 1997]

The Washington Theatre was at 11th Street west, south of Pennsylvania Avenue. The Varieties Concert Saloon was at 9th Street west, corner of C street north. The editor was not successful in locating backgrounds on these two theatres.

There were many courts-martial related to the theatres of Washington, DC. Pvt. Samuel J, Carpenter, 1st Connecticut Light Artillery was AWOL in civilian clothes, attended a performance at the Canterbury and then went to a "house on West Street in Alexandria." William A. Lynch, Veterans Reserve Corps, had been in the hospital for a year when he slipped away from his sick bed to go to the Canterbury heater. Pvt. John Hobson, 2nd Pennsylvania Light Artillery, went AWOL to visit "Canterbury Hall."

Surgeon Henry Armstrong, 2nd New York Heavy Artillery, was a general disgrace. Officers were not to be seen with public women, but he escorted Lucy Hart, madam of a whorehouse at 27 Pennsylvania Avenue, to Grover's Theatre. He used a medical corps ambulance for this outing. Later, back at Hart's "house," he got in a fist fight with a young lieutenant. First lieutenant Patrick S. Early, 13th Pennsylvania Cavalry, was drunk and obnoxious when he tried to force his way into Grover's Theatre without a ticket. In the disruption, he shot another lieutenant in the neck. Pvt. George M. Doner, 28th Veterans Reserve Corps was guarding three prisoners. He took them into a saloon next door to Ford's Theatre, where one prisoner escaped.

Five members of the 50th New York Engineers, went AWOL from the Navy Yard to "attend the [unspecified] theatre:" Charles Price, Joseph Young, Daniel Barnes, Charles Goodwin, and Floyd Moulton.

Sixteen-year old Pvt. Charles Williams, 3rd US Infantry, forged a pass to visit the theatre. Pvt. Homer H. Storing, 15th New York Cavalry, was gone three months. "I went to the theatre." Pvt. Randall Hart, 7th Michigan Cavalry, told the court, "I thought we had time to go to the theatre and not be missed." Pvt. John Morris, 7th New York Heavy Artillery, was AWOL one day. "I put on citizen's clothes to go to the theatre." Second Lieutenant Benjamin Andrews, 1st Connecticut Artillery, went AWOL to visit a theatre on King Street in Alexandria.

Clearly, Washington, DC's theatres were a vital part of the life of its citizens and its visitors, both military and civilian.

CHAPTER 8
WHITE BORDELLOS

Prostitution was no secret in Civil War Washington, DC. The provost marshal's office compiled two lists, one for seventy-three places of white prostitution and a separate list for twelve places of African-American prostitution, the latter entitled "Coloured Bawdy Houses."

The following list of white "houses" contains three columns. The first lists the name and address of the madam; the second column gives the number of inmates in the establishment, while the third column is a quality rating, ranging from first class down to "very low." "Houses of assignation" were most likely locations where a couple could rent a bed for a short period of time.

1. Miss Lucy Hart *21 Pa. Av.*   4   1
2. Madam Miller *51 Pa. Av.*   6   1
3. Mrs. Catherine Campbell *138 24th St.*   5   2
4. Madam Bennett *148 F St.*   7   ?
5. Mrs. Louis Turner *446 19th St (?)*   5   1
6. Lizzie Miller *corner 18th & E Sts.*   6   2
7. Mollie Turner *62 C St.*   3   1
8. Hattie Farwell *28 13 ½ St.*   2   2
9. Ellen Wolfe *494 13 ½ St.*   4   3
10. Miss Mina Bowers *478 13 ½ St.*   6   3
11. Mrs. Sarah Duncan *473 13 ½ St.*   2   2
12. Miss Maggie Murphy *282 D St.*   6   1
13. Sally Murphy *286 D St.*   6   1
14. Mary Taylor *298 D St.*   6   low
15. Mollie Mason *287 D St.*   7   1
16. Miss Joe Horn *291 D St.*   7   2
17. Mrs. Mary Taylor *303 D St.*   9   3
18. Mina Bearing *309 D St.*   6   3
19. Miss Nichols *591 12th St.*   5   1
20. Louie Myers *533 12th St.*   4   2
21. Mrs. Louie Hays *537 12th St.*   5   3
22. Miss Leote Gaskill *541 12th St.*   6   1

23. Mrs. Louisa Koerner *540 12th St.*   5   3

24. Mrs. Maggie Walters *532 12th St.*   14   1

25. Mrs. Louise South *252 C St.*   6   2

26. John Sputsvists *313 D St.*   6   low

27. Eliza Gibson *531 11th St.*   House of Assignation

28. Miss Molly Florence *533 11th St.*   3   2

29. Miss Kate Walters *595 11th St.*   3   2

30. Miss Mary Miller *597 11th St.*   6   3

31. Mrs. Elizabeth Harrison *284 C St.*

                                    House of Assignation

32. Miss Annie Wilson *510 10th St.*   4   1

33. Miss Sophie Hoffman *484 10th St.*   6   3

34. Mrs. E. M. Post *487 10th St.*   6   1

35. Miss Nellie Gwinn *348 E St.*   4   1

36. Miss Jane Ross *348 E St. back*   4   2

37. Sallie Austin *500 6th St.*   9   1

38. Miss Julia Deen *12 Marble Alley*   8   2

39. Miss Nellie Mathews *10 Marble Alley*   6   2

40. Mrs. Elizabeth Harris *33 Maine Av., Island*

                                                     9   2

41. Laura Tomkins *225 B St. Island*   2   3

42. Mrs. J. Rhoades *474 Maryland, Island*   6   very low

43. Mrs. E. M. Mark *473 Maryland, Island*   2   very low

44. Mary Hall *459 Maryland, Island*   18   1

45. Elizabeth Harley *4 Maryland, Island*   3   1

46. Hattie Mills *2nd near Maryland, Island*   3   3

47. Ann Benton *Tin Cup Alley, Island*   5   3

48. Mary Hessler *513 3rd St., Island*   5   3

49. Mary Murrey *493 3rd St., Island*   6   very low

50. Miss Mary Donnelly *339 C St., Island*   3   very low

51. Sarah Brown *rear of 339 C St., Island*   5   very low

52. Margaret Wilson *rear of 339 C St., Island*

                                       3   very low

53. Mrs. Roland *250 F St., Island*   4   4

54. Margaret Hanks *Fighting Alley, Island*   6   low

55. Matilda Wade *Fighting Alley, Island*   6   low

56. Mrs. Johnson *640 7th St.*   3   low

57. Ellen Hall *434 Virginia Ave., Island*   6   1

58. Mary Tolson *G St. near 1st St., Island*   3   very low

59. Catharine Dinkloker *4th at N Sts., near Navy Yard*

                                       6   3

60. Rachel Rappider *574 9th St. near H St.*   5   very low

61. Mary Conklin *95 Pa. Ave. near 10th St.*   5   very low

62. Julia Fleet *444 3rd St. Fox Hospital*   6   very low

63. Emaline Bateman *N St. between 11th & 12th*

                                       2   2

64. Margaret Venerable *249 10th St.*   4   4

65. Louisa Sanford *corner 3rd & L Sts.*   4   1

66. Eliza Foster *rear N.J. Ave. & C St.*   1   3

67. Mary Jacobs *rear N.J. Ave. & C St.*   1   3

68. Emma Howard *rear N.J. Ave. & C St.*   5   3

69. Philamena Preston *331 G St.*   3   3

70. Mrs. Weldon *497 10th St. between G & H Sts.*

                                                  2   1

71. Mrs. Wiggons *Corner 1st & B St., Island* 6 very low

72. John Muntz *512 N.J. Ave.*   (not recorded)

73. Annie Jones *195 Pa. Ave. near 10th St.*   5 very low

Missing from this roster are three establishments that appear in Chapter Three. They are: the very low class John Taylor's Rum Mill and Bawdy House at F St. near 20th St.; Annie Finnegan's very low class Rum Mill and Bawdy House at F St. near 20th St.; and "Headquarters," a Rum Mill and Bawdy House mentioned in soldiers' letters. It was at 552 12th St. and was rated 4th class.

COMMENTS

There is much to be gleaned from this simple roster. First and most obvious, the business of prostitution was codified and registered, if not actually legalized. Madams and the total number of prostitutes was known. Were there unattached streetwalkers? Probably, but a woman choosing to work in this field would have been far safer in the supervised bordellos listed here. In Washington DC today there is prostitution, illegal, unlicensed, and often dangerous. Various criminal elements force young girls into "the life."

The rate of diseases is high. Is this an improvement over the Civil War era?

Location seems important in this roster. Houses south of the Tiber Creek/Canal, i.e., on The Island, rank lower. The provost marshal rated quality on a six-point scale: 1st, 2nd, 3rd, 4th, low, and very low. The average score for non-Island houses was 2.5, half way between 2nd class and 3rd class. Houses on the Island had an average score of 4.5, half way between 4th class and low class. Tales of degraded and dangerous life on the Island seem verified by these figures.

There are interesting locations where "houses" are clustered together, such as on D street, with Maggie Murphy, Sallie Murphy, Mary Taylor, and Mina Bearing. Perhaps researchers could use GIS (Geographic Information Systems) to find out why. There were two "houses" on Marble Alley, which is now the site of the National Gallery of Art. Madams Sallie Austen and Julia Deen had a bitter rivalry, documented in *The Story the Soldiers Wouldn't Tell*. These issues were of no consequence to the soldiers and tourists of the 1860s, but they promise rewards to the historians of today who are willing to dig deeper into the history of our capital.

CHAPTER 9
"COLOURED BAWDY HOUSES"

This is the wording of the provost marshal's list of African-American bordellos. There is no indication as to whether the color designation applies just to the prostitutes or to the clients or to both. As in chapter eight, the first column contains the name of the madam and her address, the second column the number of prostitutes in that "house," and the third column is the quality rating of the establishment.

1. Julia Thomas 480 13th St.   4   3
2. Two Houses *rear of 348 E St.*   4   4
3. Misses Seal & Brown 13 *Marble Alley*

                                           6   low
4. Theadosia Herbert *Tin Cup Alley*   5   1
5. Rebecca Gaunt *Tin Cup Alley*   4   2
6. Sarah Wallace *Tin Cup Alley*   5   2
7. Sophia Harbour 489 3rd St.   2   1
8. Selia Higgins *rear of 339 C St.*   5   2
9. Josaphine Webster *Fighting Alley* 12 low
10. Biloy Becket 243 *E St. near 3rd St.* 5 low
11. Levinia Pergins 352 *Virginia Av.* 3   2
12. Emily Brown *H St. near 20th St.* 6 low

COMMENTS

Three of the bordellos were on Tin Cup Alley, also known as Willow Tree Alley. Pvt. Alfred Bellard, a member of the provost guard, inspected the off-limits alley on "Tiber Island" in late 1863 and described it as "occupied by white and black, all mixed up together on the principal [sic] that you pays your money and takes your choice." Bellard's vivid description forms part of a lively narrative, edited by David. H. Donald.

While the location of "Fighting Alley" has escaped this author, one might imagine daily (and nightly) life in Josaphine Webster's whorehouse, with its twelve prostitutes and a rating of "low." This was another establishment that the provost guard soldiers never entered except in force.

Do the alleys still exist? Yes and no. By the 20th century they had evolved into a warren of residences and small businesses. Prostitution was a minor part of this culture, yet reformers, do-gooders, and puritans in Congress (which still controls the District of Columbia) mandated that every alley house be vacated or torn down by July 1, 1944. World War II extended this deadline until June 30, 1955. In that decade gentrification had set in and many alley dwellings were now tidy middle-class (and upper middle class) homes. The new alley dwellers enlisted a ghost of the Civil War, Maj. Gen. Ulysses S. Grant III, as their advocate and Congress dropped the mandate. Today, no one lives in an alley. The same passages now have pretentious titles, such as lanes, courts, rows, and mews. The ghosts of the old alley dwellers may now be having a quiet laugh.

As to Tin Cup Alley, it was part of the Willow Tree Alley Complex, in the interior of block 534, bounded by 3, 4 ½, B, and C Streets, and Maryland Avenue Southwest. In the map, it is emphasized in a black border.

Virginia

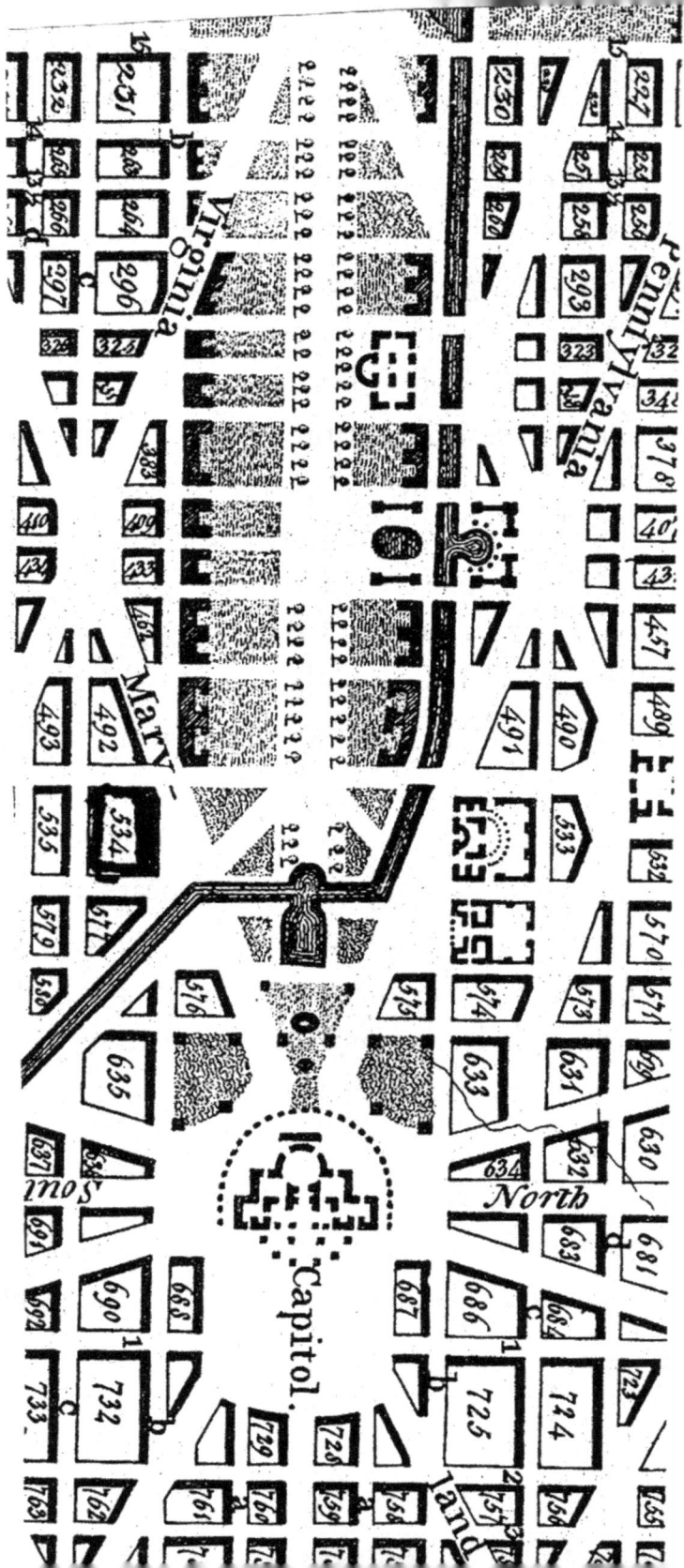

Pennsylvania

Mary[land]

Capitol.

North

Sou[th]

land

CHAPTER 10

THE WAGES OF SIN

At many Civil War events there are demonstrations of medical care. One of the common offerings has a pretend surgeon doing a pretend leg amputation. This is a great favorite with young boys, whose sense of the macabre is well developed. Indeed, in the actual war there were thousands of amputations, and the demonstrations are informative. However, it is very unlikely that re-enactors will demonstrate the symptoms or treatment of the 73,382 cases of syphilis and 109,397 cases of gonorrhea reported in white Union soldiers.

There were 421 known prostitutes in Washington DC in 1864. The good book, in Romans 6:23, tells us that "... the wages of sin is death ..." There is no way of knowing which of these cases of venereal disease were contracted in Washington, DC, but we do know that the nation's capital was the site of something unusual – a hospital devoted entirely to the treatment of sexually transmitted diseases—the Ricord Hospital. Why Ricord? In the 1860s Philippe Ricord, a Paris physician, was the world's leading authority on VD. He treated not only ordinary citizens, but in the course of his career he received decorations and medals from the royal houses of Spain, Greece, Portugal, Italy, Sweden, Luxembourg, Russia, and Belgium, presumably because members of all these noble houses had syphilis. That great American, Oliver Wendell Holmes called Ricord, "The Voltaire of the pelvis."

(If the treatments available then were not efficacious, it is possible that the next generation of kings was addled by tertiary neurosyphilis, with the resultant confusion and paranoia that set off the colossal stupidity of the First World War.)

Leaving aside such speculation, the records tell us that the Ricord Hospital was located at "Mass. Ave. corner 14th west." While the records are contradictory, the hospital's location would probably be at today's

1407 Massachusetts Avenue, near Thomas Circle, an elegant location now, but in 1864, the avenue and its neighborhood was a sea of mud, bogs, and copses. The records and their location at the National Archives are summarized in the author's book *Civil War Venereal Disease Hospitals*, published in 2014, along with studies of Confederate VD hospitals. Not for the squeamish are the details of the *surgical* treatments of syphilis.

A brief glossary may be necessary. Phymosis / phimosis is a narrowing of the prepuce/foreskin so that it cannot retracted to expose the glans/head of the penis. Corona glandis is the widest part of the glans. Condylomata are wart-like skin lesions of advanced syphilis, often quite extensive. Indurated is hardened. Hypertrophic is overgrown. Chancre is the typical syphilitic skin lesion, often circular, with a hardened edge and soft purulent (pus-like) interior. Suppuration is the formation of pus. A bistoury is a sharp surgical knife. A director is a metal probe used to steady a structure being cut. A serrifine is a small, delicate spring-loaded clamp to stop bleeding.

Pvt. Lyman Pender, 76th New York, was admitted with phymosis, perforation of the prepuce, condylomata, gonorrhea, and a greatly swollen penis. Under chloroform anesthesia the prepuce was divided from the perforation to the orifice. With the glans revealed many condylomata were removed, using scissors. Three weeks post-operation, the prepuce, now indurated and hypertrophic, was removed with a knife, again under chloroform, and six sutures were applied to unite the mucous membrane and the skin. The deep-seated condylomata which could not be removed by surgery were cauterized with nitric acid. He was returned to duty five months after admission.

Sgt. Henry Martin, 57th New York Infantry, was admitted with phymosis caused by chancres on the margin of the prepuce. The prepuce was not swollen. Using no anesthetic [!] he was circumcised and the wound closed with three sutures. There was considerable pus afterward. When the pus drainage stopped, he was returned to duty.

Pvt. P. M. Cadro, 12th US Infantry, was admitted with diagnoses of congenital phymosis, syphilis, and a bubo in his left groin. The elongated and constricted portion of the prepuce was steadied between two pairs of forceps, and the division made with one stroke of the bistoury. The mucous membrane was then divided with blunt pointed scissors, and the muco-cutaneous edges united by interrupted sutures. There was no mention of anesthesia.

There are detailed records of seven similar surgeries, but the three presented here should suffice in conveying the work of the Ricord Hospital and the suffering of its patients. It is also a reminder of the joys of penicillin.

(An obituary appeared in the Times of London, October 23, 1889, page 9.)

Our Paris Correspondent telegraphed last night :— "Dr. Philippe Ricord, the oldest medical practitioner in Paris, died this morning. He was born on the 10th of December, 1800, at Baltimore, where his father, a shipowner, had settled on being exiled by the Revolution. The grandfather was an eminent doctor at Marseilles. In 1820 Philippe Ricord came to France with his brother Alexandre, who died in 1876, and who had made botanical collections for the Jardin des Plantes. Both brothers became doctors. Philippe was appointed surgeon to some Paris hospitals, and acquired a high reputation by his treatment of certain diseases. In 1862 he was appointed physician to Prince Napoleon and consulting surgeon to the Emperor. For many years in difficulties owing to carelessness about money, he eventually, on his friends managing his purse, became prosperous. He was present at the Versailles Centenary last May, when his great age made him a striking figure, and a few weeks ago he ascended the Eiffel Tower. He came over to Paris from Versailles on the 6th of October to vote for the Republicans, and then caught cold from having to wait on the platform for a train. This caused his fatal illness. He was the author of numerous medical treatises.

CHAPTER 11

NASHVILLE, TENNESSEE

Why Nashville in a book about Washington, DC? These two cities were major transit points for tens of thousands of Union soldiers. Their similarities and differences may help form a perspective on the joys and snares for tourists and soldiers alike in the two locations.

The 1860 census shows a non-slave population of just 14,000, barely a city by today's standards, but it was a major cultural center, with a university, a medical school, several excellent high schools, and two dozen publishers. The busy steamboat landing was supplemented with the newly connected telegraph and a railroad bridge over the Cumberland River. Floating above the city was the newly completed state capitol, in the Ionic Greek style.

The war was a year away, but busy commerce has already spawned an industry of welcoming arms: 207 women told the 1860 census takers that their occupation was "prostitute." There was the elegant "house" of Rebecca and Eliza Higgins, at 101-103 North Front Street, with seventeen prostitutes, six schoolchildren, two pre-schoolers, a carpenter, a brick mason, and a black man named Tom Trimble. Most of the establishments were far less elegant, and many of the public women were desperately poor widows with small children.

A few high points from the 1860 census may illustrate the relevant records. Charles and Sarah Healey lived together. He was 26; she was 22. His occupation "coach painter." Hers was "prostitute." Jane Ross, age 26, and Letha Ross, age 16, lived at the same address and were listed as "prostitute." John Tanley was head of household, at an address which he shared with Mary Quillin (30), Sarah Moore (19), Jane Hill (18), and Mary Brown (17), all of whom were prostitutes. At adjacent addresses were Mary Wanton (27), Martha Brown (28), Amanda Smith (20), Jennie Rogers (26),

Eliza Rogers (19), Frances Baker (21), and Mollie Wilson (21). They, too, told the census taker that they were prostitutes.

Right behind the Union soldiers, with money in their pockets, came another army, women from up-river and downriver, eager to share the wealth. In weeks after the Union troops arrived, the original 207 soiled doves (as the newspapers called them), were joined by hundreds more. Soon VD was felling more men than Rebel bullets. The US Army quickly set up an innovative and successful system of legal prostitution, with inspections and treatment. But private enterprise had already come to the rescue for those who feared the authorities or did not qualify for the army's program. By serendipity, a complete copy of the July 7, 1865 Nashville *Daily Union* was found by Beverly A. Lowry during research at the National Archives. The paper is in excellent condition and yielded safely to Xerox copying. Much of the advertising was of mundane matters: shoes, bread, crackers, steamboat tickets, window glass, mattresses, millinery, even lost and found.

But more relevant to the soldiers, who had little need for furniture and millinery, were ads from doctors offering to cure syphilis and a multitude of other conditions. In many ways, Civil Was society was more honest and less prudish than today. Can one imagine the ads which follow appearing this year on the front pages of the Los Angeles *Times*, or the San Francisco *Chronicle*, or the New York *Times*?

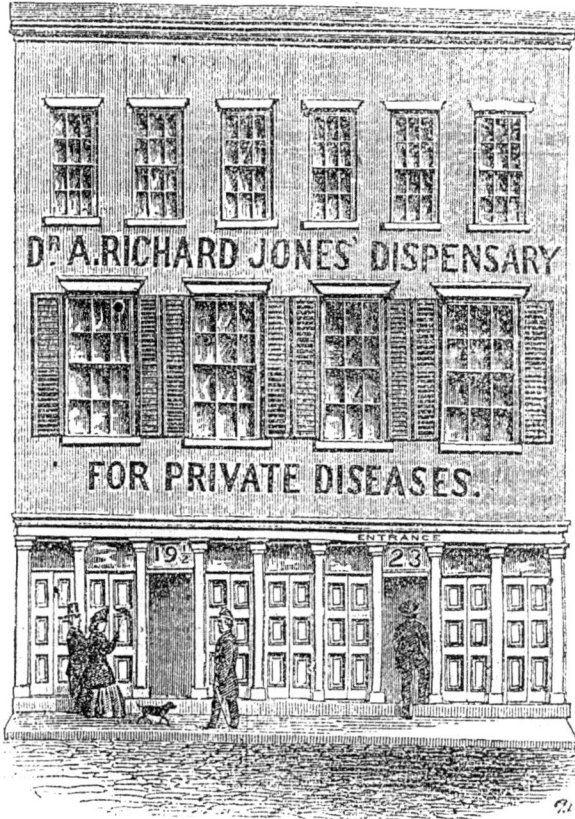

NO. 23 DEADERICK STREET,

HAVING FOR SEVERAL YEARS PAST NOTICED THE BARBAROUS MODE OF TREATMENT for **PRIVATE DISEASES**, by the use of caustic applications and caustic jections, with painful operations, etc., was aroused to the presumption that these diseases might cured by some more pleasant and reliable remedies, as by the

Old Course of Treatment

Physicians are constantly annoyed by patients returning with secondary symptoms. Dr. Jones has covered a mode of treatment for these diseases which is rather a pleasure than a pain. His treatm has undergone a thorough investigation, and has been found much more efficient than any other... is never troubled with the complaints of patients with secondary Syphilis, swollen organs, or with many symptoms produced by the Old School Treatment.

Dr. Jones' charges are the same in all cases—will charge the same for one week's attention that would for one month, and it is of course to his interest to cure a case as speedily as possible.

MEDICINES FURNISHED

in all cases, which saves to the patient the extravagant prices of medicines or prescriptions, which in many cases, cost more than the whole of his charges, besides you save yourself the probabilit exposure, in calling for the medicines at a Drug Store. The office is so arranged that none need you while there. All business and correspondence **Strictly Private.**

To my patrons I am happy to state that I have been enabled to secure the services of

DR. A. KING,

as associate Physician, who will, in my absence, attend all my patients. DR. KING is perhaps oldest Venerial Surgeon in the United States, having devoted his attention to this popular branch of the Practice since 1825, and I take pleasure in recommending him to the public as one well qualified for the arduous duties of the profession.

DR. KING is the only person in the country, except myself, who thoroughly understands the use o my Medicines, and with his long experience no one more reliable in difficult cases can be found. Pa tients, calling at this Dispensary will therefore have the advice and treatment of both Dr. K. and my self, or either, as may be desired, without extra charge.

CHAPTER 12
WALKING D.C. TODAY

———————————

The past is never dead. It's not even past.
—William Faulker

Let us begin at the Smithsonian's National Gallery of Art, East Building. After absorbing as much contemporary art as you need, take the stairs down to the underground moving walkway that conveys you west to the lower floor of the classical works of the main gallery. As you glide through the dimly-lit tunnel, close your eyes and fly back 150 years. You'll find your-self in the tulgey cellar of Miss Julia Deen's house of prostitution. Although it may be lively and riotous above, as her eight whores and numerous customers engage in the Rites of Aphrodite, the cellar, so near Tiber Creek is damp and reeking of mildew. A good place to store wine, but no place for humans.

Now the moving belt has deposited you in the main gallery. Exit into the sunshine, walk a short block to the north, and turn left on Pennsylvania Avenue. Go past the Federal Trade Commission and the National Archives, then pause in front of the Department of Justice. You will search in vain for the bronze commemorative plaque that should be there, if Washington did full justice to its history. What would such a plaque tell us? Surely we would read of Sophie Hoffman, and her six "girls," Annie Wilson, who kept four "soiled doves" under her protective wing, and Mary Conklin and her five soldiers fighting the War Between the Sheets.

On to the next block, which houses the Internal Revenue Service. There John Sputsvists (his name spelling has many variations) kept six women. Next door was the establishment of Mollie Post, who had three girls ready to welcome visitors. One more bordello occupied this block, that of Mrs. Post with her stable of six women.

The Trump International Hotel is next on Pennsylvania Avenue. This block was a cornucopia of concupiscence, with five whorehouses. Seven bawds worked for Miss Jo Horn. Mary Taylor's house was rated "low," and it is likely that her nine inmates lived in unhygienic squalor. Mina Bearing engaged six women to serve her clients, and Louise Koener had five women who, like most Civil War whores, probably died young of disease or alcoholism. The final Trump location madam was Maggie Walters. With her fourteen Cyprians, Maggie had a veritable fornication factory. (Why Cyprians? In Greek legend Aphrodite arose from the waves at ancient Cyprus.)

The next block houses the current Postal Service. This block was even more bawdy than the one preceding it—nine bordellos with a total of forty-six prostitutes. One mentioned in Civil War writings was the Wolf's Den, operated by Ellen Wolfe. The last block on the Pennsylvania Avenue tour is now occupied by the Ronald Reagan Building. This huge edifice also lacks a bronze plaque, one which would memorialize the four madams active there in 1864 (Hattie Farwell, Maggie Murphy, Sally Murphy, and Mollie Mason) and their stable of twenty-women who could be rented for riding, or in the words of one Civil War diarist, "horizontal refreshment."

Tired of prostitution stories? Go west a few more yards to the White House, then called the Executive

Mansion. If you had visited in October 1864 you would have seen First Lieutenant Arthur W. White of the Union Cavalry Light Guards milking a cow on the White House lawn. This may have been unauthorized, but what got White in real trouble was tormenting the President's cows by tying cups, pans, and buckets to their tails, which made them run about wildly and reduced their milk production. The Lincoln family, with small children, needed the milk. White's regiment was organized in Ohio and sent to protect the President. The lieutenant's antics provided no visible protection. He was booted out of the army.

About "hookers." They were <u>not</u> named after Gen. Hooker. While he was a wild man, a poker-playing, hard-drinking bachelor, the term hooker meaning prostitute, probably originated many years earlier in New York's harbor, where a peninsula, Corlear's Hook, was famed for its women of ill repute.

Away from Pennsylvania Avenue, there was no shortage of *nymphs du pave*. At today's National Portrait Gallery, Rachel Rapidder had five girls. Close your eyes at the Department of Agriculture building and you'll see Miss Nichols' five girls, and at Metro Center, careful excavation would have disclosed the remains of Philamena Preston and her three girls. The list seems endless. Union Station has Eliza Foster, Mary Jacobs,

Emma Howard, with a total of seven girls. On a quiet night, you might catch the sounds of tearful regrets as young girls, far from home, had another drink of whiskey and met the next stranger. Farther afield, at the Botanic Garden, was Hattie Mills and her three "boarders," and Mrs. Wiggons, whose six inmates were probably not botanists.

These tales of commercial debauchery, should be lightened by a human interest story, and here it is. Private Benjamin Culp, of the 11th Veteran Reserve Corps, was a patient in a DC hospital. When arrested, he was in his bed, drunk, smoking a cigar. In bed with him were two prostitutes, also drunk and smoking cigars. When the police arrived, the three made "gestures prejudicial to good order and military discipline."

Civil War Washington was deeply involved in that conflict, working to manage strategy, medical care, soldier's pay, pensions for the wounded and the widows, and raising the money for the millions of rations, rifles, cannons, horses, wagons, and steamboats needed to fight a continent-wide war. But always there was the usually unmentioned human side, the part that called to visitors, whether they be military or civilian. Hopefully this walking tour will add to the history of the capital of the free world.

APPENDIX

First, a *caveat,* Those who wish to delve into the murky waters of Washington, DC misbehavior during the Civil War must have time, patience and good eye sight. And a joy in reading old hand-written documents. The National Archives on Pennsylvania Avenue has thousands of cubic feet of records that have never been made into a searchable database, or digitized in any useful form. Here is how to find them.

Begin with the "Union Provost Marshal's File of Papers Relating to Individual Citizens," which is numbered File M345, and consists of 299 rolls of 16-millimeter microfilm. On the screen will appear photographic reproductions of odd-sized hand-written documents, arranged alphabetically by the names of those arrested or investigated. If the researcher knows whose record he (or she) seeks, and can find that person, and that person's code number is in M345, he can then turn to the next source.

That source is the 94 rolls of 35-millimeter microfilm that forms M416, "Union Provost Marshal's File of Two or More Names Relating to Citizens." The code number in M345 is the key to M416. None of these M416 files are arranged by type of crime. To be a productive effort, this diligent researcher should read every one of the 393 rolls of film, recording name, date, and type of offense and placing the findings into a database such as Access or Excel. The final result would a boon to all future researchers and a treasure trove for historians and graduate students.

The next source to survey is the Turner-Baker Index. Major Levi C. Turner was appointed associate judge advocate for the Army in August 1862, with jurisdiction over the District of Columbia and northern Virginia. Turner's job was to find and arrest disloyal citizens, draft dodgers, and army deserters.

Lafayette Baker was one of the more colorful and controversial characters of the Civil War. He was a various times a spy, a secret agent, a special provost marshal, and colonel of the First District of Columbia Cavalry, a unit formed to enforce Union rule in Washington, DC. Baker and his men investigated crooked contractors, slave stealers, smugglers, conspirators, defrauders, vandals, and traitors. Altogether, Turner and Baker investigated over 8,000 cases.

After the war, in the years 1869 and 1873, the files were combined into the Turner-Baker files, and alphabetized. One might say semi-alphabetized. All the names beginning with the same letter were grouped together, but not alphabetized within that letter group. Thus, to find "Wolsey" one would need to go through the entire "W" file. And "W" names are very common. It is slightly helpful that within each letter group, the files are in chronological order.

We are not done. In the early years of the war, cases of treason were investigated by the State Department, often in secret, with the files sequestered. State Department records are held at a different Archives location, in College Park, Maryland.

The diligent soul who would make all these files into to one master database would need to start at an early age, avoid tobacco, red meat, and excess alcohol, and always wear his seat belt. Choosing long-lived ancestors would also be helpful. If he should falter, a look at Frederick H. Dyer's massive two-volume *A Compendium of the War of the Rebellion* will strengthen his resolve. Dyer did this work by himself eighty years before the invention of the computer.

SOURCES

National Archives, Washington, DC. Record Group 393,
Volume 298, Provost Marshal's Department of
Washington, 22nd Army Corps, 1864-1865.

Boyd, Andrew. *Boyd's Washington and Georgetown
Directory, containing a Business Directory*. 1864.

Borchert, James: *Alley Life in Washington*. University of
Illinois Press, Urbana. 1982.

Burlingame, Michael, and John R. Turner Ettlinger. *Inside Lincoln's White House – The Complete Civil War Diary of John Hay.* Southern Illinois University Press. Carbondale. 1997.

Donald, David H.: *Gone for a Soldier – the Diary of Alfred Bellard.* Boston. 1975. Page 256.

Lowry, Thomas P.: *The Story the Soldiers Wouldn't Tell.* Stackpole Books, Mechanicsburg, PA. 1994.

Lowry, Thomas P.: *The Civil War Bawdy Houses of Washington DC.* Sgt. Kirkland's Press. Fredericksburg, VA. 1996. (Contains a 24 by 36-inch map showing the location of the bawdy houses.)

Lowry, Thomas P.: *Confederate Heroines.* Louisiana State University Press, Baton Rouge, LA. 2006. (Includes discussion of researching provost marshal records, pages 182-184.)

Lowry, Thomas P.: *Primrose Path: A Biblical-Sociological Study of the Ladies of the Evening in Civil War Richmond and Washington, DC.* Amazon & CreateSpace. 2011. (Contains every known fact about every known prostitute in both capitals.)

Lowry, Thomas P.: *Civil War Venereal Disease Hospitals.* Amazon & CreateSpace. 2014.

Idle
Winter
Press

www.ingramcontent.com/pod-product-compliance
Lightning Source LLC
Chambersburg PA
CBHW071553040426
42452CB00008B/1159